FOUR BALLS AND
WALKING

FOUR BALLS AND WALKING

Walking with Power and Peace

BY

RICHARD R. GUERRA

TATE PUBLISHING *& Enterprises*

Published by Tate Publishing & Enterprises, LLC
127 E. Trade Center Terrace | Mustang, Oklahoma 73064 USA
1.888.361.9473 | www.tatepublishing.com

Tate Publishing is committed to excellence in the publishing industry. The company reflects the philosophy established by the founders, based on Psalm 68:11,
"The Lord gave the word and great was the company of those who published it."

Book design copyright © 2008 by Tate Publishing, LLC. All rights reserved.
Cover design by Leah LeFlore
Interior design by Lindsay B. Behrens

Published in the United States of America

ISBN: 978-1-60604-131-4
1. Biography & Autobiography: Personal Memoirs
2. Inspiration: Motivational: Biography & Autobiography
08.05.13

DEDICATION

This book is dedicated to my God, my Holy Father Jesus Christ, who gave me life, more than once. Who gave me the peace to endure the darkest nights, and who carried me when I was weak, until I had the power. I write this book by His request and guidance for His glory.

To my mother Carmen and my father Ruben who are in heaven. To my brother David and my sisters Sandra, Cindy, Jerry, Margo, and Becky and all my family who loved and cared for me when I needed it the most.

To the many doctors and nurses who kept me alive.

To my many friends who gave the support needed so I may continue to strive.

And to my loving wife, Michelle, and daughter, Aria Rose, I give my love.

> The cords of the grave coiled around me; the snares of death confronted me. In my distress I called to the lord; I called out to my God. From His temple He heard my voice; my cry came to His ears.
>
> II Samuel 22:6–7

ACKNOWLEDGEMENT

A special thanks to Alice Armstrong for assisting in editing.

TABLE OF CONTENTS

INTRODUCTION

Some days, time crawls tortoise–like; other days time dashes away as fast as a jackrabbit. Moving slowly or quickly, time never stops, but constantly alters the course of our lives. Not even the wisest or the strongest of men can do anything to suppress this flow. We just try to comprehend the moment we're in and await the moment to come.

On October 28, 1975, at the age of nineteen, I lost life as I knew it. In a flash I was thrust onto a new course of life without a chart, without directions. Obstacles littered my path, but my will to survive would triumph.

Fresh out of high school I needed a job. Dressed in a long woolen trench coat, iron–creased slacks and polished shoes, I pondered the gas station marquee: "Full time mechanic needed. Apply within." Without any knowledge of cars or experience as a mechanic, I applied. The manager asked, "Are you a mechanic?"

"Would I be applying if I wasn't?"

"Be here at six a.m. You have the job."

The first task of the morning involved driving the boss' truck. Upon backing out of the garage, I tore off the passenger–side mirror. The boss glared at me.

"Hey, I'm sorry. It's early. Give me a break," I said. Two weeks later, even though the restrooms were always sparkling and the tire racks were always arranged neatly, I was fired. I guess cars trailing oil down the street gave the boss good reason.

"Kid, you're a great guy, you work hard, but you don't really know anything about cars, do you?" asked the boss when I turned the lug nuts on a European car the wrong direction. "You need to be in a business that deals with people, but not this business. Good luck," he called as I walked away. Once again I was desperately seeking work.

Fortune smiled upon me a couple of weeks later when I heard that a beverage manager at one of the largest country club hotels in the area needed a top–notch bartender. For a few weeks I practiced the art of mixing and serving cocktails. Then, dressed in a three piece suit, I applied.

"I hear your looking for a bartender," I said, looking the manager in the eye. "Yes I am. Are you a bartender?"

"Well now, would I be applying for this job if I wasn't a bartender? In fact, I'm so good that I'll work for free behind your main bar for three days. If after three days, you don't think, I'm one of the best, I'll leave," I offered. Three days later I was hired to work the main bar, a position for only the experienced and best. What a job! Working with beautiful waitresses, wearing three piece suits and patent leather shoes, carrying $100 bills in my pocket, I was flying high. The other bartenders envied me, a seventeen–year–old high school graduate. It's not my fault they never asked my age, nor would they find out, at least not for eighteen months. In only three months I was promoted to beverage manager. Gold–plated pens adorned my pocket. A nametag embossed *Mr. Guerin* adorned my lapel. I was top dog and I couldn't be stopped; I was in the fast lane, I had the power. More than eighteen months of wine, women, song, and immoralities too numerous to mention went by before I was to know true power: the power of God.

FROM THE DARKNESS
INTO THE LIGHT

October 28, 1975, days before ghouls and goblins roamed the streets, my buddies and I were hosting a Halloween party at my apartment complex. After most of the guests had left, we cleaned up, took a hot sauna and raced to the pool for a quick dip. Upon seeing Kurt dive into the pool, I anticipated feeling that cool, refreshing water envelop me. I dove into the pool, but the refreshing coolness I expected was not what I felt. Instead I felt fear followed by panic. Why? I knew I was in the water, but why was I frightened? What could harm me here? Then I realized I couldn't breathe. Some force was clutching my body pulling me down to the murky depths of the pool.

Fight, struggle, anything, my mind screamed. *You must have air, you must have that precious life-giving air!* Through the blur of the water I saw Ralph standing at the edge of the pool, looking at me. I do not know if I cried out for help. What force kept me bobbing up and down I do not know. I do know God helped me.

The sound of my name reached my ears.

"Rich! Rich! I'm coming," Kurt called. Then his arms were around me as reassuring as a mother's touch. For the moment I was safe, but safe from what? What was causing this agonizing fear? I sensed no physical pain. Is it not pain that warns you of danger or injury? What was it?

Kurt dragged me from the pool. I lay flat on my back on the concrete, staring up at the amber lights overhead. I felt a puzzling sensation, one I had never experienced before. My legs seemed to be hovering over me. I could see Ralph at the end of my body, though I wasn't raising my head.

"Ralph," I cried, "where are my legs? Are they lying flat or hovering in the air?"

"They're lying flat," he answered. With that I closed my eyes and heard: "You're paralyzed. Your legs are paralyzed. You cannot walk." I didn't know then but I know now that it was the Holy Spirit letting me know this.

I felt no remorse or sorrow at the time, just an understanding in my soul. I thank God for the power and peace He gave to me at that moment, a reassurance and a power that were more comforting than I could have imagined. A belief in His power and grace that I had never known, nor wanted to know living the lifestyle I had chosen, washed over me.

> And call upon me in the day of trouble: I will deliver thee, and thou shalt glorify me.
>
> Psalms 50:15 (KJV)

"The ambulance is here Rich. Everything's going to be okay now," I heard someone say. But no matter the extent of my injuries, I was alive and knew I would stay alive no matter what. For at that moment, like never before in my life, I felt my Holy Father with me, holding my hand, reassuring me. I just waited calmly, silently for the EMTs. Then, once again panic struck. I couldn't breathe.

"I need air! I need air!" I screamed while that drowning feeling swept over me again. Gasping for air, I called out to the paramedic standing over me, "I can't breathe! I can't breathe!" The paramedic didn't move. "Why aren't you helping me?" I yelled frantically. "I can't breathe. I can't breathe!" Still he didn't budge. "Why aren't you helping me? Can't you hear me screaming for air?" Still he didn't move.

Then, as if through a tunnel, I heard Kurt yelling angrily, "Help him! Can't you see he needs air? Help him!" Shock set in. I wasn't breathing and the paramedic was doing nothing. He was going to let me die. Why? At that moment Kurt dropped to his knees and gave me artificial respiration. Darkness crept over me. In the darkness, that reassuring voice from deep inside my soul said, "Go to sleep now, and don't you fear. I am with you, and you are safe." I sighed a great breath and fell into a deep sleep knowing that there was a God, and He held me in his arms. He brought me from the darkness into the light.

> What time I am afraid, I will trust in thee. In God
> I will praise his word, in God I have put my trust;
> I will not fear what flesh can do unto me.
>
> Psalm 56: 3–4 (KJV)

ONLY A DREAM

I awoke disoriented, as if from a life–like dream.

"Hello, son. You're all right. You're in the hospital. Everything's going to be all right," my mother crooned. I felt her gentle, reassuring touch caressing my face.

My father, his voice strong, said, "Mi hijo, you're going to be okay!" I saw the tears in his eyes though. I had never before seen my father cry

"Oh God, please give them the strength you've given me," I prayed.

The room was dark, lit only by equipment constantly monitoring my vitals. Beyond the foot of my bed I could see the desk where a nurse was in constant readiness to react to any sign of danger. A tube snaking down my raw throat connected to some sort of pumping machine. Intense pain plagued both sides of my head, which still haunts me on damp rainy days. Later I learned the source of this pain was traction tongs resembling those used to carry large blocks of ice screwed tightly into my skull. I also wore a device resembling some discarded Frankenstein relic strapped around my head to keep my neck stable.

A nurse notified the doctor that I was conscious, and he soon appeared in the doorway. Dr. Handley was a tall, strong, confident–looking man, and instantly I had faith in him. He had a reassuring smile on his face, yet a serious look in his eyes.

"Can you feel this," he asked, as he pricked my foot with a pin. I wanted to say yes, but I knew this wasn't true.

"No," I grunted. He moved further up my leg.

"How about this?"

"No," I could see now his hand on my chest.

"How about this?" I still felt nothing.

"No, No."

I'm sure it pained Dr. Handley to have to say the next words, but not as much as it pained my father and mother to hear them. You see the pool I had dove into was not full of water, as you would expect. We were not informed that the city had closed down the facility. And that they had demanded the door to be locked and posted. Neither had been done.

"Richard, you have severed your spinal column which has caused full paralysis. It is a critical situation, and we must operate immediately, or you will not survive. I don't know at this time how much movement will return," he said.

"I know," I replied. I recall a strange look of amazement in his eyes. But I knew, yes, I knew.

God had already told me. God, whom I never worshipped, God whom I never thanked, had comforted me in my darkest hour and eased my fear. I closed my eyes to once again sleep and dream. It's good to dream because dreams answer your questions, but sometimes the answers aren't what we want to hear. Then they are painful. Sometimes the truth is painful. I began to dread the nights because my dreams were true and painful. I wanted to get out of bed.

Silently, I lifted myself, watching for the nurse knowing that she would not allow this. Slyly, I moved to a position where I readied myself to spring for the door and escape. Just as I was about to leap, the nurse pushed me back down on the bed. I struggled to escape, but she held me firmly.

"Let me go. Let me go," I screamed. Yet she held fast. "I don't need to be here. Why won't you let me go?" Without uttering a sound, she released my wrists but kept circling the bed blocking my escape. I tried to push past her, my arms and legs flailing. Again she grabbed my arms and held me down so I could not escape, or was it to stop me from further injuring myself?

"Rich, Rich, wake up," called the nurse. "It's okay," she cooed. I awoke with tears in my eyes, and knowledge in my heart. I would never escape. Ever. It was only a dream.

> For thou art my lamp, O Lord: and the Lord will
> lighten my darkness.
>
> II Samuel 22:29 (KJV)

LOOK WHAT I DID

As night turned to day and day to night, seconds felt like minutes and minutes like hours and all the horrors of the accident overwhelmed my soul. In a mere seventy–two hours my life had completely changed.

How can this be? Why did this happen? All the planning and scheming to be Big Dog, the Boss, ended by a dive into a pool. *This can't happen to me; I'm Mr. Guerra.* Just four days ago I had moved into an upscale loft apartment. One day before that I was rooming with three high school friends in an apartment above a bar. They did not know about the double life I was leading. No one knew. I told myself they wouldn't understand. The truth was I feared they might unmask me, expose my charade.

Just three days earlier as an eighteen–year–old, eleven days shy of my nineteenth birthday, I had made love to a beautiful thirty–something woman in my loft apartment. Then I had gone to work where I was the manager overseeing five different lounges, several restaurants, and all staff. Professional men and woman, all of legal age to serve alcohol never knew they were working for a mere teenager. Now they would know.

"Richard, you have a visitor," my mother said. As I watched this gorgeous woman approach, my heart sank. She was one of many with whom I was having affairs. As she entered the room, tears streamed down her cheeks and horror filled her eyes. She approached my bedside.

"Richard, I love you. I'll never leave your side," she promised as she bent down to kiss me. I turned away and closed my eyes.

How could she want to kiss me? Doesn't she see the shape I'm in? Can't she see the tubes running down my throat and the metal device strapped to my head? The smell of her perfume, a scent that until now intoxicated and excited me, nauseated me.

"I don't want you here," I said coldly. "Don't ever come back. I can't be with you or anyone else. Get out. Get out!" I yelled.

Crying, she ran from the room. My father and mother watched in shock. Not only were they trying to understand how their young son could be so cold–hearted, but also how he could be involved with this mature woman. They had to wonder what I had been doing for the last year.

In that moment, I recalled my interview for the bartending job. How smug I had been thinking I really put it over on them. I didn't even own a white dress shirt or black slacks, the required attire. Nor did I have the money to buy them. So I borrowed a shirt that fit a little too snugly and pants that were long enough if I wore them low on my hips. Dressing for the job was the easy part.

The lodge was some ten miles from where I lived. I had to be at work promptly at four p.m., and my shift ended around one a.m. I needed this job, so being late was not an option. Yet it happened and I was called into the manager's office. There I stood, an eighteen-year-old punk with Buddy Holly glasses and shaggy hair. I couldn't afford a haircut. The general manager and his most voluptuous assistant looked me over and then asked why I was late.

Now what could I tell them? Certainly the truth would not do. They would never understand that a bartender working at their fine lodge, in the most prestigious bar, was late for work because he didn't own a car.

"My car broke down and I had to walk over ten miles," I lied. "I'm here right? Only a little late. If you're around about two o'clock tonight maybe I could hit you up for a ride? But if not, don't worry about it. I got it covered. What do you think?" My saving grace was that I was wearing their monogrammed vest and my shoes were shined. My father had taught me guys with *sharp* always have shined shoes, and man it worked.

"Hey Rich, sorry man. I just had to make sure you were going to show. You sure you have a way home? You know I'm off-duty now and we're leaving."

"No problem. I'll catch you guys later. I have to get to the lounge."

"Thanks for getting here, man," called the manager as I strutted away, Big Dog.

Three months later I was promoted to beverage manager. Yeah, that's right, beverage manager. By then I had money. Between salary, tips, and what I ripped off, I was bringing in close to a grand each week. I figured if they hadn't figured me out by now, they would never catch on. I had it all, big money, and all the bobbles, beads, and babes I could handle. I wore three–piece custom suits, Italian silk socks, and patent leather shoes. *I could be running this joint by the time I'm old enough to drink.*

For the next year I drank only the oldest scotch and the finest wine. Not only could I afford it, but I figured I was worth ever penny. After all, I was Big Dog.

One night while perched upon my reserved bar stool overseeing my domain, keeping ever–watchful eyes on the bartenders and waitresses for sticky fingers, a call came from the front desk. A voice said, "Mr. Guerra could you please come up front. There is a gentleman here that says he's your father."

"I'll be right there. Make sure that my father is comfortable until I get there," I ordered. Looking back, I remember standing behind my lavish desk, my father sitting across from me in the tall–backed chair, and asking him, "Would you like a cocktail or something? I'll call for it." Man. I was so wrapped up in this game I had forgotten who I was. I was Mr. Guerra, right?

I knew my father well and I knew he would play the game. He wouldn't blow my cover. We visited. I gave him a tour. Then, upon saying goodbye, he looked at me. "I hope you know what you're doing," he said.

"Don't worry, dad. Look around. I got it covered. Can't you see? Look what I did."

> For he cometh in with vanity, and departeth in darkness, and his name shall be covered in darkness.
>
> Ecclesiastes 6:4

CAN'T

What a word: Can't. It means you're not able to, or you're not supposed to, do something. If you use this word long enough, you will become comfortable saying "I can't!" At least I did. This simple word affected me more than I ever imagined it could. Here I was trapped in a hospital bed, my once virile body now motionless. "You can't breathe using your lungs. You see you're paralyzed. But you don't have to do anything. You're on a respirator. Your diaphragm will take over," my doctor said.

I learned during my time in the hospital to have great respect for the human body; it is a great machine with two of most everything in case one part is lost or falters. Unfortunately, it has only one spinal column. This vital column houses all the nerves, which send messages to the brain, which creates movement. I had damaged my spinal column so that my nerves could no longer get through to my brain; instead they got a constant busy signal. "Because you smashed the third, fourth and fifth vertebra, you are now a quadriplegic, paralyzed from the neck down, you can't feel anything," the doctor said matter–of–factly.

This can't be. That would mean I could never again take a woman into my arms and make love to her. I'm the Big Dog. They have to be wrong, I thought. I tried to explain to the nurses that they were wrong, that I could feel. Something was pinching my back, and it hurt.

"No, Rich. That's just your imagination. You can't feel anything," the nurse said. I didn't believe her. I knew the sensation of pain and I knew I felt it then.

"Okay Rich, we'll check. See there's noth…oh my. You're right. The mattress is bunched up. We've smoothed it out for you, okay! But, really you can't feel it. You can't move your legs. You can't move your arms. You can't move your hands. You can't move your fingers," she said to humor me.

You can't, you can't, you can't. No reason to try, you can't. So, I didn't.

> And it shall come to pass, that before they call,
> I will answer; and while they are yet speaking I
> will hear.
>
> Isaiah 66:24 (KJV)

I awoke in the wee hours of the morning, dreadfully thirsty. I looked around and saw my sister, Margo.

"What do you need Bro? I'll get it," she offered, and I knew she would. She loved me.

"Water please, give me some water," I whispered. I waited, anticipating that cool refreshing drink.

"Here, Bro! Here's your water."

I waited. She held the glass in front of me, but out of my reach. I looked at her in disbelief. What was she doing? She knew I couldn't grab the glass.

Is she getting back at me for some prank I perpetrated upon her in our childhood? How could she do this? Where are Mom and Dad? They'll put a stop to this.

"Bro, if you want a drink, grab the glass," she ordered, "You can do it. Grab the glass."

Grab the glass, what does she mean? She knows I can't grab the glass. Why is she torturing me this way, I wondered. Since the moment of the accident, my heart had slowly been filling with despair and bewilderment. Suddenly it all turned to anger.

"I can't grab the glass," I yelled. No sooner had these words left my mouth than I felt a cool sensation running over my wrist and down my arm. It was water, water flowing from the broken plastic cup I held in my hand.

And there was no more *can't*.

> Thy right hand, Oh Lord, is become glorious in power; Thy right hand, O Lord, hath dashed in pieces the enemy.
>
> Exodus 15:6 (KJV)

WHAT NEXT?

In a moment, I realized that the word can't means I don't want to or don't believe I can. I was starting to hear, to see, to believe. In my youth, God had sent messages in my dreams, but I did not hear them. He sent angels to protect me, yet I did not see them. Why should I? I didn't want His guidance. All I cared for and all I worked for was money. Greed and lust were my masters, until I faced this life–threatening crisis. Then I called out to God to save me. But why? God did not ask me to break my neck in order to have His love. He had already given me his love. He gives his love to all of us. All He asked was that I believe that Jesus Christ was His only Son, that He sent His only Son, who died on the cross, to show me, to show us, His love. Now I know all things are possible in God's plan for me.

The next morning I awoke to see Dr. Handley standing by my bed.

"Good morning, Richard. How are you feeling?" he asked, gazing at me with those serious penetrating eyes.

"Doc, I know I am paralyzed, but what's next?" I asked.

"Well," he replied, "you're going to be here in intensive care for a while.

Then when you're already, we will send you to a rehabilitation center so you can work at becoming the best you can be in a wheelchair. It's going to be hard, but I know you can do it."

Suddenly disbelief washed over me again. Until now I had never seen anyone in a wheelchair except for Raymond Burr in *Ironsides*. Certainly I had never personally known anyone in a wheelchair. The challenge ahead of me was formidable, one that I was too tired to face now. I would have to face it eventually, but not now. I closed my eyes and returned to dreamland.

Some time later I awoke to see a strange woman standing beside my bed.

"Hello Richard. My name is Karen. I'm a physical therapist. I know you have suffered a terrible accident, but you're going to regain your strength."

Can't she see the condition I am in? Why doesn't she leave me alone? She took my hand and slipped a ring on my finger. Attached to the ring was a rubber ball small enough to fit in the palm of my hand.

Karen whispered in my ear, "Squeeze this all the time you lie here Richard, and don't you stop. Be strong and live." She gently kissed my cheek and walked out the door. I wanted to call out to her, but I couldn't muster the strength. I didn't know how to react, but my subconscious knew that she was right. As I drifted back into sleep, my hand squeezed the ball. The squeezes were imperceptible at first. Then the nights turned to days and the days to nights, and I grew stronger.

> Consider the work of God: for who can make that straight which he hath made crooked?
>
> Ecclesiastes 7:13

My hand, like rooster talons gripping a fencepost, closed around the ball. I know I can feel it. I know I can. I concentrated harder than I ever had before, just to make my hand follow the command to squeeze a ball. I counted, *one, two, three, one, two, three,* as I tried to squeeze.

"Look. Look," I cried. My father stared at my hand. "Did you see that? It moved. Look. Watch." *One, two, three.* I squeezed my eyes shut looking at my fingers with my mind's eye, feeling them at the end of my arm. Oh! God please let them move. *One, two, three.*

"There, see." And like the flick of an inchworm the tip of my finger moved. Oh! What joy filled my heart. To move no matter how slightly was a miracle. To think, this minute accomplishment was of epic proportions. I would never stop now.

My past no longer existed. Like a newborn baby, I had no fear. I was open to all God's wonders. I faced a new beginning. "Son! You keep moving all the time. You keep moving. I know it hurts, but you can take it. No matter how hard the task, no matter how powerful the pain, you must endure," said my father in his strong voice. And pain did come. What next?

> Blessed are those who endure when they are tested. When they pass the test, they will receive the crown of life that God has promised in those who love him.
>
> James 1:12 (KJV)

SHAKES AND ROCK CANDY

So many times we forget how much the little things matter. We worry about petty concerns like if we have all the material possessions needed to be recognized as a success. When times are good we pat ourselves on the back for a job well done. Ohhhh! But when trouble comes and times are hard, we curse God and ask, "Why me? I don't deserve this. It's not right." I am no different than others in this regard. In my youth, I congratulated myself for my successes, but blamed God for my failures.

Time as I had always known it ceased to exist as did the past. Certainly none of Big Dog's running mates were hanging around. The future, the unknown, loomed in front of me. Every tick of the clock, every labored breath, every moment of existence was new. I didn't know what the future held for me, but I was grateful to be alive.

Sugar water dripped into my veins, sustaining my life, and I was glad, but as the number of foodless days mounted, I longed for solid sustenance. Lobster tails, T-bone steaks, cheeseburgers with onions, and coffee with pie ala mode were what I wanted and what I thought

I needed. Then one day, through the whirs and hums of the many machines monitoring my vitals, I thought I heard someone ask me if I wanted a milkshake. Am I dreaming? Is someone asking me about a chocolate shake? As I focused my eyes, I recognized Dr. Urmana standing beside me.

"Well how about it! Do you think you could handle a chocolate shake?" he asked. *Me! Drink a chocolate shake? What is this, a pop stand? I am Big Dog. I drink Champagne cocktails, snifters of brandy, fine wines, 50–year–old Scotch. This is what players drink. What kind of joke is this? Real funny, if I could move I'd show you how funny!*

Then I remembered; I'm not Big Dog anymore. A chocolate shake, sure I can handle one. I nodded with my eyes, but I guess Dr. Handley couldn't read eyes.

"Well, maybe in a couple of days we'll see how you're doing, okay! But for now, how about some hard candy? Would you like that instead?" he asked.

I relished water and hard candy like they were rare delicacies. When sour hard candy was added to my diet of a sugar water drip, I was as pleased as if I were dining in the world's finest restaurant. And to think I could have as much as I cared for. Man! I was living. For a brief moment I was happy and peaceful, but this too would pass.

"Rich, you've developed a pressure sore," a nurse informed me. "We are going to switch you to a different bed. You just lie there, and we'll take care of everything." Just lie here? Like what else am I going to do? Head out to the nearest nightclub and wow the women on the dance floor with my Travolta moves? The nurse rolled me out of the room. As we neared our destination, a wave of apprehension washed over me and for good reason I would soon learn.

The nurse wheeled me into my new room and introduced me to the Stryker bed. Now, I have never found out if the bed was named for a real Dr. Stryker who invented it, but if it was, I sure would have liked to meet him. First I would have thanked him for his invention and then I would have punched him right in the mouth.

The purpose of this contraption is to allow for easy turning of patients in fragile condition without moving them. Picture this if you will. The bed looked like an oversized hamster cage wheel in which a long thin army cot was suspended between iron rails. The cot was just big enough for me to lie on, but not comfortably. First, the nurses laid me on my stomach. My arms hung over the sides of the cot and the metal–rimmed edges pressed firmly against my shoulders. Then they buckled thin canvas straps in place to support my forehead and chin. I was to remain in this position for weeks.

Now, I'm quite sure that whoever devised this contraption had all good intentions and used the most comfortable materials available in the early seventies. However, as the patient strapped into this bed, it felt like a medieval torture device. To this day I shudder at the thought of this bed and turn away if I see one.

When I was a kid, every morning I thought I dreaded hearing my mother say, "Richard, wake up. It's seven o'clock. Time for school." But I didn't know then what it really means to feel dread.

The Stryker bed inspired true dread. Every few hours a nurse would pop in my room.

"Richard, it's time to turn you. Ready? We are going to turn on the lights." This turning produced pain worse than any I could ever have imagined. The first time was the worst. I was lying on my back, perfectly comfortable, when a force of nurses marched into the room. They proceeded to strap an olive drab army cot on top of me and lock it in place. I became a Stryker sandwich. Then the fun began. Wheeee! On this first ride I had no idea how it was going to be or how my body was going to react, but I sure didn't like the looks of it. They turned me slowly, my head rising towards the ceiling. I felt like I was riding the scariest of roller coasters as I reached standing position. Now, my body had not been perpendicular for weeks, and it didn't react well to being vertical once again. Through blurred vision I saw my mother and father watching, and I wished with all my heart that they could stop this ride. As I descended, my face closing in on the floor, vomit spewed from mouth. I cried out in pain, and then I passed out cold. When I came to, I felt like I had been turned upside down and inside out.

Words cannot describe the pain that accompanied these turnings of my ruptured body. Of course I did not resent the nurses for my pain, but I hated those nurses' words: "Richard, it's time." And I heard them every two hours for weeks. Perhaps my pain was like that of a tortured prisoner of war. I admire and praise their strength to endure. Only moments after my return to consciousness, I realized that the coming weeks were going to be a test of my will, my newfound love for God and my belief in his power.

> What time I am afraid, I will trust in thee.
>
> Psalms 56–3 (KJV)

Fifteen minutes after being turned face down, new pain struck me. My arms hung over the sides of the cot and the iron rails bit into my shoulders. Dead weight, I was unable to shift to relieve the pain. Then an even more intense pain stemming from the thin hard canvas straps supporting my forehead, arrived. The pain was relentless, a never–ending reminder of where I was. No amount of foam padding protected my shoulders or forehead from developing large sore welts.

Every two hours, twenty–four hours a day, I was turned. Some days into this ordeal sleep deprivation began to torture me too and I finally broke down. My family came to the rescue. They helped me to survive and keep my sanity by doing little kindnesses for me. My dear brother David shaved me, whether I needed it or not, to keep my mind off the pain. He talked to me in his gentle voice reassuring me that it would be all right. I still remember his tender touch. My sister Margo would lie on the floor underneath me to brush my teeth and sometimes caressed my face until I slept. Without them, I honestly believe I might have gone mad.

Strangely, when I think back, I do not recall the arrival of the day when I no longer had to take this ride. Isn't that how we are? When times are rough, we pray to our God for help making promise after promise, but when all is well, we forget the suffering and the vows we made. However, I have never forgotten the little acts of mercy that got me through my darkest hours. To this day, whenever I'm just not sure what to do, I shave and brush my teeth. Then I remember how I endured the worst with the help of God's love and I know that nothing is impossible if I believe. God gives us miracles every day. They are the little things, like shakes and rock candy.

> Heal me, O Lord and I shall be healed; save me,
> and I shall be saved; for thou art my praise.
>
> Jeremiah 17:14 (KJV)

ONLY A TEST

Oh! Glorious were the days in the weeks following my release from the torment of the Stryker bed. It's said that those things that don't kill you will make you stronger, and I guess I have to agree. Surely nothing could be worse than the horrendous pain I had endured while being rolled. I had faced and overcome the dreadful time I spent rolling, and I knew I was a much stronger person for suffering. Or was I?

> Blessed be God, which hath not turned away from
> my prayer, nor His mercy from me.
>
> Psalms 66:20 (KJV)

The doctors upgraded my condition from critical to stable. For a few short hours each day, I was transferred from the bed to an oversized recliner with wheels. This little movement and different positioning of my body was the beginning of the road to physical therapy. A sign on the door of the physical therapy room read, "If it's physical its therapy." This moving forced my muscles to work, especially and most importantly my lungs. Just like an infant, I was breathing from my diaphragm. I watched my stomach rise and fall with each labored breathe. Although it was not easy, I was breathing.

Once I was situated in the recliner, the nurse clipped an emergency button to my shirt.

"Okay Richard. If you need anything, you press the button and we will be right here. If you can't press the button just pull on it and an alarm will sound and we'll be here as fast as lightning. Don't you worry," the nurse assured me. I had complete confidence in the staff and myself. Because of my rubber ball, I was able to press the button when I needed something. Many times I pushed the button and without fail they came.

Rarely was I alone in my room. A family member kept me company most of the time, but one night was different in many ways. I had just finished my evening routine. The caring nurses had washed me and settled me for the night. As always they asked if I needed anything before they left to continue with their many chores. I must have been exhausted because I fell asleep before they left the room.

Sometime later I awoke with a startle. *Oh no, not again. This can't be happening again. God help. Help me. I can't breath. I can't breath*! I couldn't call out and even if I could they wouldn't hear me. *The button. Press the button. Press the button. That's all you have to do. Just press it. Oh no, where is the button? Oh God, I'm so afraid. Oh God, where is the button?* I struggled, looking about and there it was! My lifeline. All I had to do was press it, but I couldn't. The call button hung on the wall an arm's length from the bed. The nurse had forgotten to clip it to my pajama top. Terror consumed me. *I can't breathe! I can't reach the cord! Oh God, let me reach this cord!* I lifted my arm, reached for the cord, and took my last breath. Then I went away.

The journey I took amazes me to this day. I journeyed outside of my body. Hovering in the ceiling corner, I looked down at my lifeless body. *Well Rich, you are out of here. Time's up. Last call.* Then I heard, "Code Blue! Code Blue!"

My, my. Look how fast they run. Wow, what a lot of commotion. Where are they going? Hey look. They're coming into this room. They're all around me. Well what do you know? I'm Code Blue. Huh, isn't that something. Doctors yelled orders and nurses followed them. *But hey, I'm up here. Can't you see me? I'm up here. Oh my, they're cutting into my throat. I better get down there to see if I'm okay.* I looked up from my bed and saw their faces. They all wore the expressions of soldiers victorious in battle.

Someone spoke to me. "Hey Rich, are you with us? Can you see me? We thought we lost you for a minute there, but you're okay now." With wide eyes I looked about. I raised my eyes up to the ceiling. I was no longer there! A doctor leaning over me must have read the fear and disbelief in my eyes.

"Richard, you quit breathing. We had to cut a hole in your throat to open your air passage," he explained. Then the nurse who had settled me for the night cradled me in her arms. Her tears dripped onto my shirt.

"Richard, I'm so sorry. I don't know how I could ever have made such a mistake. Please forgive me. Thank God you were able to reach the cord and pull it out of the wall. But how did you do it?" Without answering I closed my eyes and fell asleep. In my sleep, I cried, because I knew what I had seen and I knew where I had been, but I did not understand.

Was my vision true? Had God saved me? I didn't know, and this uncertainty frightened me. I did not yet know how great God's powers are, nor had I ever wanted to know. I wanted to believe that I, a mere man, was all–powerful. I wanted to believe that I and I alone controlled my destiny. I wanted to believe that I chose the path I walked. How wrong I was. Still, I didn't understand why these things were happening to me. Was I so evil that God was punishing me? I did not know.

What I did know was that the horrible memories of the days and nights that I rolled on the Stryker bed seemed far away, only to be replaced by horrible memories of choking. I hope that you, my dear reader, never have to experience this procedure. Just to imagine it is quite unsettling. There I lay with a small opening in my throat, a tracheotomy. A small rod was inserted through the thin membrane in the base of my throat. The trache tube made it impossible to speak although I learned that if I covered the end of the tube I could make some sound

This tube, vital for my survival, was not without a cost. That old choking feeling was back in a new and improved form.

Every so often, throughout the day and night, a nurse would enter my room carrying a thin plastic hose that connected to a small vacuum. This is when the fun began. While apologizing, she would insert this vacuum cleaner into the trache. I would choke and gag for the minutes it took to clear the airway. While my airway was blocked, my body would convulse violently, like one possessed by evil spirits. I despised this procedure, but without it mucus would build up and asphyxiate me. Once again, I had no control over my fate, something I was not used. However, I was beginning to get the message. It was either do this or die again.

I didn't understand at the time, but God had different plans for me than I had for myself. He made these plans for me well before my natural birth. And while I speak of God's power now, I had to endure many more tests before I accepted God's love for me. Now, however, I know that regardless of the tests I face throughout my life here on earth, in the end God's will for me is to receive eternal peace, love and hope, and freedom from all pain and sorrow, freedom from Stryker beds and vacuum cleaners. All I had to do was believe. It was only a test.

> In God I will praise his word, in God I will put my
> trust; I will not fear what flesh can do unto me.
>
> Psalm 56:4 (KJV)

THREE-MINUTE EGG

Through all the darkness, through all the pain, through all the despair, in the far reaches of my mind I saw a light. This light warmed my spirit and kept me from thinking about the past darkness. I reached a time when I could see the future, and I began to prepare for it. I still had a lifetime to go, but I wanted to crawl, and I was not afraid to fall. Not anymore. Thoughts of being able to move forward filled my mind. Just to do it! Just to breathe, just to sit up, just to eat, just to do it.

Never having had children of my own, I did not understand new parents' amazement at the smallest acts or achievements of their infants. How they cheered with delight when their babies gurgled their first words or how they laughed with delight when their little ones sat up for the first time wobbling to and fro, or how they admired their toddlers when they managed to get their little spoons to their mouths. Never mind that they left more food on the floor than they placed in their mouths. Oh! So much joy from such little feats of strength. Now here I was, an infant in a man's body, longing to complete these feats of strength.

Once I learned to breathe on my own without too much difficulty, the nurse removed the trache. Generally, this experience is not a humorous one, but it was for me. In fact, dear reader, as you continue on this journey with me there will be plenty of times when we will laugh through the tears, and that's okay. Sometimes being able to laugh eases the load of hard times, and while tears help to cleanse our souls, laughter helps to mend our hearts and keeps us believing in the joys of life through the darkest hours.

To finally be rid of this hideous breathing apparatus imbedded in my throat was surely a reason to rejoice. I waited anxiously for the doctor to arrive. They had promised me that it would be removed this evening. *Where is he? They said tonight. Come on what's taking him so long?* Finally, in walked the nurse with towels and rubber gloves, a good sign. Surely the doctor would soon follow. As she prepped me, I wondered how they were going to do this in the bed. *Maybe she's just getting me ready to go to surgery.* As she placed a towel on my chest, I started to worry. *What the heck does she think she's doing?*

As she reached for the tube in my throat, she said, "Okay Richard, here we go! Are you ready? I'm going to pull it out on the count of three. One, two—"

"Hey! Hey!" I lunged toward her keeping my body close to her so she couldn't pull the tube out. "Are you crazy? You can't just pull it out! You'll cut right through my neck! My head will fall off! Where's the doc? You're nuts. You've lost your mind?" I yelled. She looked at me like I was crazy.

"Richard, what makes you think that your head will fall off?" she asked.

"What kind of nurse are you? Don't you know that there is a wire inside my throat running from one side of the tube around my spinal column and attached to the other side of the tube? If you pull this tube out you will cut my head off!" I told her. She started laughing. Now I'm always up for a good laugh, but I really couldn't find any humor in being decapitated.

"Richard you silly, there is no wire in your neck. The tube is just held in place by a small piece of tape," she explained as she removed the tube. And guess what? She was right. My head didn't fall off. After she cleaned the wound and taped over the hole, I started to laugh, and laugh I did until I cried. Being able to breathe once again on my own was pure joy. I had always taken breathing for granted. Now it was an amazing feat.

> Sorrow is better than laughter: for by the sadness
> of the countenance the heart is made better.
>
> Ecclesiastes 7:3 (KJV)

Without a doubt, the days were getting better. I took deep breaths without fear and looked forward to sitting up. Though I was going to be sitting for the rest of my life, I was thrilled to be sitting now. Little feats, little strides filled the days of my life. I was thrilled with the anticipation of eating real food. Sitting in my oversized leather throne, feeling the warmth of the sun shining upon my face, I smiled like a kid on Christmas. Today, I would dine. Yes, the nurse had called down to the kitchen and requested the finest cuisine be sent to my room. Oh the joy! A few moments later, a darling aide arrived, carrying a tray adorned with a silver, covered platter. She lifted the cover, and there it sat like the Hope diamond, an unshelled three–minute soft egg.

I'm not sure, but I would bet I was drooling like a hungry dog. As the nurse cracked the shell, I'm sure I saw a glow of light or probably just the egg yolk. The time had come to eat food, real food, glorious food! I licked my chops and waited for her to scoop this heavenly morsel into my mouth, but she stopped.

"Oh no, you're not eating this. How could they be so ignorant? And they call themselves cooks. They can't even make a proper egg. I'll be damned if I'm going to have you eat this slimy thing for your first meal. Over my dead body. Don't worry Rich I'm calling right now. They will bring another one, and it better be right this time," she warned.

Now let me tell you, if I had been able to move, her body would have been in a prone position on the floor and that egg would have been sucked down my throat like a bowling ball through a vacuum tube, shell and all.

Speak about heartache, I prayed that the next one would be right; but it took three tries for the cooks to meet the nurse's expectations. As the saying goes, anything worth having is worth waiting for. This egg was worth waiting for. It was truly the finest three–minute egg.

> For this cause I bow my knees unto the Father of
> our Lord Jesus Christ.
>
> Ephesians 3:14 (KJV)

SKY

"The *love* I lost was a *C–note*," was a great song for the times. Characterized by disco music, hot pants, tight bell–bottoms and Quianna shirts, the seventies were pretty wild. But I wouldn't be dancing disco or wearing flashy clothes. In fact, I hadn't worn clothes of any kind for more than thirty days. And there was no reason to. Who would care? Who would be looking at me? Certainly not women. I was sure no woman would ever again be attracted to me.

Doubt again darkened my thoughts. How could this be? How could I, Big Dog, face a future devoid of sexual intimacy? With limited movement I would forever be incapable of satisfying a woman sexually. Pain, sorrow, regret welled up in my heart at this realization. Of all the losses I experienced, the loss of my manhood hurt the most. After all, I was Big Dog.

Once I had realized how easily I could manipulate women, I did it often. I had no shame and no morals. My own physical needs, satisfying my insatiable drive, had topped my list of concerns. But now, now I had nothing to look forward to, nothing to offer. What would I do? How would I ever be able to accept this? What would I do? What would I do?

Once again in my darkest hour God knew my despair. Were He not the loving God He is, surely He would have turned from me in scorn, and I would have deserved it. But instead of turning His back on me like I so often had done to Him, God sent an angel to reassure me, an angel in the form of a beautiful woman named Sky.

Late one evening my father was standing vigil in my room. All the commotion of the day was subsiding and I was waiting for the night nurse to prepare me for bedtime. As I lay there, really doing nothing more than staring into space contemplating disheartening thoughts, a nurse entered the room. Though I didn't recall ever seeing her before, she must have attended to me before because my father acknowledged her. I ignored her as she went about her nightly routine. She drew my attention before she left, though.

"Your son is a very handsome man," she said to my father. Then to my surprise, she bent down and kissed me. And this kiss was no, *Hey, you're a nice guy everything is going to be okay keep a stiff upper lip* kiss. No, this kiss said, *How are you doing big boy? Do you want to come out and play?* She whispered in my ear, "Richard, I love you, and when you get out of here we're going to go out together. You better hurry up and get strong. I'm waiting. My name is Sky."

Let me tell you, thinking about that kiss still gives me shivers to this day. How great God is. Even when I don't believe, even when I don't call out to Him, He knows my despair. As she walked out of the room, my father and I exchanged that knowing look and silly grin that the attention of a pretty woman always induces in men.

Am I dreaming or did a beautiful woman just come on to me? I was not dreaming. This woman had just ignited a spark in me that would never be extinguished again, a spark that would flame and forever more burn in me, a flame that inspired me to grow stronger every day, a fire ignited by God to save my soul. The hope of love was upon me strengthening me every day. What a miraculous thing love is. It can build up the weakest man. We should thank our God every day for such love because without the hope of love, we walk in darkness and suffer a loneliness that can destroy our very being. In a brief moment my life, once again changed. I was given a reason to continue, to strive, to believe, to hope and to dream, to reach for the Sky.

The day finally arrived when I was strong enough to leave the hospital for a few hours. In these few hours I would be in the company of a beautiful woman, a woman who without knowing was surely sent by God to save my soul. In the past year I had no trouble being with women. I was in no way intimidated or nervous when sharing intimacy with them. But this night was different; my confidence had been shaken. I felt like a teenager going to prom on his first date, something I never experienced. In high school I thought the prom was for kids, not a player like me.

Tonight I was going on a date with Sky, but like Cinder*fella*, I had no clothes to go to the ball though I had been wearing a gown for weeks. Many suits hung in my closet, but they were much too large for me now. I experienced a *Leave it to Beaver* moment discussing my dilemma with my father. I had to depend on him to buy a suit of clothes for my date. Fortunately, I trusted my father's taste; he always dressed sharply, himself. He didn't let me down. The outfit consisted of a pair of rust colored, large check slacks, a silk, large collared shirt, a General Patton–style short jacket, and a perfectly matched pair of shiny cordovan shoes. It was a strange sensation to have my father dress me like I was once again a young boy, but I didn't mind, not one bit.

As I lay waiting for Sky to arrive, dressed to the nines, I wondered about the night to come. You wouldn't believe how scared I was of the unknown. I knew I was going to have to contend with many changes. First, I would have to depend on others and on devices for things I had always before done for myself. I even needed a device in order to urinate. It seldom worked causing enormous embarrassment. I would have to overcome that humiliation. I would have to overcome having people look at me with pity. I would have to overcome the inaccessible world that I was venturing into. And I did. I had to believe I was still a man. And I did! I partied with Sky and her friends that night, and for a few hours I felt like a man again. All because of Sky.

> He hath delivered my soul in peace from the battle
> that was against me: for there were many with me.
>
> Psalm 55:18 (KJV)

MARIONJOY

The care and tenderness the hospital staff gave me throughout the initial stages of my journey was incredible. To me, all nurses were angels put upon this earth to watch over the maimed and afflicted. To recognize them and honor them after the great Florence Nightingale is most appropriate. When the pain was so great I wanted to give up or the nights were so long I thought morning has ceased to exist, the nurses were there to comfort me, with a touch as loving and caring as my mother's. I found this to be true in every stage of my rehabilitation and throughout my journey into the unknown. Angels of mercy lived in my midst.

The time arrived for me to continue on the journey towards independence. I felt like a fledgling leaving the nest for the first time. I had to leave my comfort zone. On a chilly winter morning, the nurses prepared me to travel via ambulance to my next stop. They dressed me in warm clothes, a jacket and a wool cap. I remember this cap because it was the final touch in my preparation. A nurse, tears in her eyes, placed it gently on my head and gave me a kiss for luck. All those who had cared for me and saved my life gathered to wish me well and send me on my way. I will forever remember the care, the coddling, the gentle touches of all those who made my life as peaceful as possible and enabled me to withstand the pain. As I was placed in the ambulance, all warm and toasty, I looked back, blew a kiss, closed my eyes and dreamt of the past. Next stop: Marionjoy Rehabilitation Center.

"Vake up, vake up! No more time for sleep. Vake up now." I awoke from my dream expecting to see my loving nurses crowded around me. Instead I awoke to the orders of a woman I thought was surely a drill instructor left over from the Third Reich.

"Goot morning, Reechard. My name is Bonnie Von Augen. I will be your head nurse the entire time you are here." As my eyes focused, I knew I no longer was in Kansas, Toto.

I didn't know where I was, but I had a feeling I wasn't going to like it. Standing in front of me was a large, stocky, hard-nosed, redheaded angel of mercy. Or was she? *Can't I go back to where I was? I'm not ready yet.* Fraulein Von Augen took my hand in her oversized mitt and said, "Vet me see you move dees hand. I heard you moved eet." Not being in any position to disobey this direct order I waved my hand. What pleasure she derived from this little motion. "Ahh yes, wrist you have, wrist I see. Yes dats goot, ve vill work dem, yes ve vill. Now rest up because soon ve vill start. I'll be bach!"

So here I was in Marionjoy Rehabilitation Center, one of the finest physical therapy centers in the Midwest. Their slogan read, "If it's physical, its therapy. No pain! No gain!" I would soon find out how true this slogan was. For the last time, my mother helped me off with my jacket and cap, kissed me goodbye and left. I felt as the same insecurity I had experienced when she dropped me off for my first day of kindergarten years ago. I understood how frightened Helen Keller must have been the first time she was apart from her loving family and left with her instructor, Anne. There's no turning back. It's show time. Wimps get off the stage. Only the strong allowed. I guess I'm up.

I was facing three months of the most grueling physical training that I would ever encounter. I would find the strength to endure through belief in the all-mighty powers and grace of God. It amazes me to think how many lessons and gifts from God it took before my hard-headed, lame, mortal self would finally accept the fact that God is all powerful and merciful.

Some thirty years and many gifts from God later, I realize that I still strayed from His path and tried to live life on my own only to once again be humbled before Him. If only I had accepted this fact years ago as I have now, I'm sure that my journey would have been easier and less painful. Why do we do this to ourselves? God does not ask anything of us other than to love Him with all our hearts. That's simple. He did not say we had to break our necks or sacrifice our lives to have His love. Just Love Him. That's all. And believe!

The room I occupied at Marionjoy looked like a college dorm. The facility, although one of the finest, was relatively small. It housed fifty to seventy–five in–house patients. One floor was for stroke victims, another floor was for geriatrics, and the first floor was for persons with spinal cord injuries and head traumas. I would spend four months on this floor. The center, less formal than a hospital, had a positive atmosphere. It was made for working, training and mending broken bodies and minds. Qualified medical staff were on hand at all times, but if, at anytime during patients' rehabilitation programs their health relapsed, they would be transported back to a hospital. Once they were safe and strong enough they could return to continue their therapy.

My first day at Marionjoy was filled with orientation and meeting my primary nursing staff. People came and went, explaining their function and what they were going to do to help me become independent. Physical therapists would have the task of strengthening me. They would push me to continue no matter how hard the tasks or how much pain arose from them. Pain is only weakness leaving your body, they said. Occupational therapists would teach me new techniques to accomplish old feats. Tying shoes, combing my hair, washing myself, eating and maneuvering comfortably in public were all skills I needed to learn.

A psychiatrist was also on my medical team to help heal my mind. Of all the doctors, the psychiatrist frightened me the most. No one could truly know how I felt or hurt, no matter how well educated or experienced. They could only imagine. Yet these doctors and therapists believed with all their hearts that they could and would help me to become independent despite my disability.

As the day came to an end, I was totally exhausted from being poked, prodded, tested, and labeled. If I had possessed an inkling of how much hard work, pain, and suffering I would have to endure, I don't know if I would have had the strength or heart to stay put here. At the hospital I had been told only that I was going somewhere I would learn to be the best I could be and it wasn't the Army. Or was it? I would soon come to know what tough love meant. As night fell, I fell into a deep sleep. Yet even as I slept changes were happening through the night. At Marionjoy.

What time I am afraid, I will trust in thee.

Psalm 56:3 (KJV)

THE ARRIVAL OF PEGASUS

Morning arrived and with it the next stage of my journey. I awoke to a sight that horrified me because it spoke the reality I was going to have to live with for the rest of my life. It was Pegasus, my winged steed. He stood against my bed; close enough I could stroke his hard, black–leather body and touch his strong, firm, metal frame. I despised the sight of him, and wished he would fly far, far away, but I knew this would never happen. He was to be my life–long companion. You see, Pegasus is my wheelchair.

Here I was, without any warning, all alone for the first time with Pegasus. *This is so cruel. Why didn't someone warn me he would be arriving?* Tough love it was, like the pain of a child when the mother had to remove a bandage. She could have pulled it slowly which only delayed the inevitable, or in one quick swipe be done with it. Yeah, that's tough love! I didn't want him here. I didn't want to ride him. *Who let him in my room? Please come take him away. I don't want him. Please someone take him away!* But no one heard. No one came. As I stared at him, I cried. Thoughts of the past came like a flood overwhelming me with despair. Never again would I be running or jumping. Never again would I be walking the walk, the strong and graceful gait that my Uncle Tootsie taught me. Never again.

Through the tears, I came to understand that I would have to learn to ride this beast, and eventually, I would fly like the wind. I would not only survive, but thrive. Once again, however, I first would have to pay a price. The cost was pain.

> Be merciful unto me, Oh God, be merciful unto me: for my soul trusteth in thee: yea, in the shadow of thy wings will I make my refuge, until these calamities be overpast.
>
> Psalm 57:1 (KJV)

In walked a group of nurses and aides. Their objective was to place me in the chair and get my body used to this position. Time to saddle up, little buckaroo. Although these women were small, they were experienced in transferring a large dead weight from a bed into a chair. I sat on the edge of the bed, and two nurses in one quick upward motion would stand me up and swing me into the chair. As I sat there preparing for this move, I felt faint, not out of fear but because my blood pressure was struggling to pump up my body, something it had not done for quite some time.

The nurses assured me I need not worry. They said if I did pass out, they would tilt my chair back allowing blood to once again rush to my head which should bring me back around. Let me tell you, it worked, and I'm glad it did because this was not the first or last time I would face this feeling of losing consciousness.

It's amazing how many different conditions may make one pass out. Sometimes people faint from sheer fright. Others faint at the sight of blood. Slamming your head into a floor, something that I would do many times in the years to come, can cause you to lose consciousness. So can a dramatic drop in blood pressure. The best cause, however, is pure, unadulterated pain. Now I'm not talking about hitting–your–funny–bone pain or stubbing–your–toe pain or even the smashing–your–finger–with–a hammer pain. No, this pain, the kind that causes a loss of consciousness, is in a league of its own, a pain so intense that every fiber of your being cries out in a blood curdling scream until you pass out. It is a pain so intense that all your senses shut down, because your mind cannot cope with it.

I couldn't see. I couldn't hear. I couldn't even cry. If my mind had not shut down I surely would have gone insane. As incredible as it may be, I soon thanked God for at least this, the temporary loss of consciousness.

No one knew what would happen when they moved me. According to the books, the most that should happen would be I'd feel a little nauseated and light–headed for a few moments. Oh! How I wished, this would have been true. Until that moment I couldn't ever imagine how painful pain could be. Even the Stryker bed didn't inflict this kind of pain. I think only being impaled with a hot rod iron from head to toe would even come close. To this day, I have never faced anything comparable, nor do I want to. As experienced and accustomed as the nurses were to seeing persons who had been hurt experience pain, they were shocked at the ferocity of pain that surged through my entire body.

Apparently, my reaction caught them off guard. I don't recall how long I was out, but the last words I heard were, "Get him back in bed. Hurry!" When I awoke, I could feel the coolness of a towel pressing gently against my forehead and see those beautiful angels staring at me, holding me, crying, and letting me know how sorry they were. And I knew that this one time was far from being the last.

"Well that was fun now, wasn't it?" I stated, much to their amazement.

The objective of this whole ordeal was to be able get to the physical therapy area downstairs. If I did not make it for my hour session, the day was wasted. I was assigned only one hour per day, and this hour was crucial to my rehabilitation process, and there was plenty of competition for the available time slots. So if I was ever to get stronger, I had to be there, and to be there I had to be in the chair, and to be in the chair, I would have to overcome this pain. As easy as this may sound, I found it was not the case. Far from it.

Although I knew how important it was to attend these sessions, I dreaded the thought of getting there. *Somehow I must fight through the pain. I must. But how?* I remembered when my father told me at the beginning of this journey, "Son, I know you hurt and I know you hurt bad. But you take it. You hear? You take it. You're my son and you have the strength to endure." So endure I did. Every time I moved to the chair, I passed out. I feared that one of these times I wouldn't regain consciousness. But I always did.

When morning came, I knew it was soon to be that time again and as the girls prepared to move me, I would close my eyes and think, *I can do this. I know this is going to hurt and hurt bad but you're a tough guy right. You can do it. So what if you scream. So what if it hurts. So what if you pass out. No matter what, you will do it. And you will do it, again and again.* I gritted my teeth so I would not scream. I counted one, two, three, go! And they would move me. Once in the morning and once in the evening, I would hurt, and I would hold back the screams and pass out.

Each day I thought the pain was a little less, but as the days turned to weeks and I continued to hurt, sometimes I thought I was just kidding myself. *How much longer can this go on? Is there a light at the end of the tunnel? When dear God? When?*

My journey exhibits the power and love of God working on me, even though I still didn't want to believe it could be. How foolish we are to doubt his glory. Twelve days into this battle, on a Thursday evening, an hour or so before I would once again face this ritual, my sister's mother–in–law, sister–in–law, and a friend came to visit. I welcomed them and treated them with respect. Blessed with the spirit and very involved in the ministry of God, they asked if it would be all right if they prayed for me. They also said that their friend was a healer in the faith, who believed that he could take away my pain through God's blessing. God would transfer the pain from my body to the healer's and the wash it away. Let me tell you, ladies and gentlemen and children of all ages, I did not believe a word this "faith–healer" said, but I was desperate enough to try anything.

As he prayed for me, I tried to believe. I closed my eyes, because that's what you do when you're praying. I listened to this stranger speak and I couldn't believe what I heard. He was not talking just to God, but also to the devil. In fact, he was yelling at the devil, telling him to release me from this pain. He said that God had sent him to take my pain and that he did not fear the pain or the devil himself.

"In Jesus' name pain will be gone and cleansed in this body through the power of God," he said. And let me tell you, if I were the devil, I would have run screaming from the room. And by God's power the devil did.

> God thundereth marvelously with his voice; Great things doeth he, which we cannot comprehend.
>
> Job 37:5 (KJV)

After I said my goodbyes to my family and their friend, I thought how nice it was of them to travel all this way to visit me, pray for me, and ask that God take the pain from my back and body. *I wonder how they knew I was in such pain especially in my back? Perhaps my eldest sister Sandra told them. Yeah that had to be it. How else could they possible know?* Even though the prayer seemed silly, it was nice that they took the time and went through the motions. Their kindness made me feel better. It's nice to know there are people who care about others even when they don't know them.

After my visitors left, the nurses came in for the evening transfer.

"All right girls, here we go again. Fun time," I joked. And ah one, and ah two, and ah scream. With my eyes closed tightly and my teeth clenched, we did the move. Whew! That's over with. Nighty–night.

The next morning I awoke anticipating the move once again. Oh yeah, here we go again. Ah one, and ah two, and ah scream. Man! I was sure getting tired of this and I could think of better things to do in the morning. After getting situated, the girls rolled me down to therapy. I had to be transferred again to the workout cots. *Here we go again.* I hated screaming in front of others and I was sure it didn't help their states of mind, either. But alas, it had to be done.

After returning me to my room this grueling morning, one of the staff nurses asked, "Richard, we have moved you three times since last night what happened?"

"What do you mean what happened? You were there. We counted, I closed my eyes and clenched my teeth, you moved me and I screamed. Wait a minute. I did scream, right?"

"Well, that's what I mean," she stated. "You didn't."

"I didn't?"

"No. You didn't. Think back." As I thought back, I realized that I had prepared for the move with my eyes closed and my teeth clenched and I had anticipated the pain that was sure to come. But I hadn't passed out. In fact, I hadn't hurt at all. Oh my!

"You remember those people that I told you came to visit and prayed with me? Well they prayed that God would take my pain, pass it through their friend and then cleanse both our bodies and rid me of all pain," I told her. Now whether or not I chose to believe God removed my pain, I could not deny the fact that I no longer hurt. *Oh my! Is it true? Is it possible that they were right, that there is a God and he can do such things?* That night I slept and I thanked God—a God I didn't know—for taking away this pain. Now I would be able to start my training. I anxiously awaited every morning with renewed power and peace. And I no longer feared the arrival of Pegasus.

> I will cry unto God most high; unto God that performeth all things for me.
>
> Psalm 57:2 (KJV)

IF IT'S PHYSICAL, IT'S THERAPY

In the absence of debilitating pain and the presence of a renewed spirit, I was able to move forward in my rehabilitation program. The first challenge was to arrive on time for my appointed therapy. You're probably thinking, "Now how hard could that be?" All I had to do was go down the hall to the elevator, about twenty five yards from my room, down one floor and there I would be, ready for show time.

The next day, after the girls positioned me in Pegasus without anyone crying because of my pain, I was ready to be taken downstairs, but the girls turned and walked away. "Hey, where's everybody going? Don't I have to be at therapy in ten minutes?" I called.

"Yeah, you do. See you down there." Out the door they went. *Okay the first test has started.* I couldn't get back in bed by myself so that was not an option, and I felt foolish just sitting there in the middle of my room. I had wanted so much to be able to do something physical, so I did. I started moving myself.

Hey! Hey! I'm moving here. I maneuvered Pegasus and aimed him toward the door. I pushed on the hard rubber pegs that extended from the rims to help me because I had no real grip yet. I soon realized this was not going to be as easy or fun as I had thought it would be. In fact, it took quite a few minutes for me to just exit the room. Then I stared down the hallway towards the elevator. Have you ever seen a scary movie in which someone is running down a hall but the hall seems to keep getting longer and longer? That's exactly what I saw: a seemingly never–ending green carpet. I pushed with all my might, yet I never seemed to go farther than a couple of inches at a time. Just to get to the other side of the hall was a great feat, let alone get down the green mile.

The girls passed me coming and going calling out, "Hurry up. You only have an hour. They're waiting for you." *Can't they see I'm doing the best I can and going as fast as I can? If they would just push me, I would be there already.* I soon had to accept the fact that this was not going to happen, not now, not ever, as long as I was in the halls of Marionjoy. *This sucks.* But onward I pushed. I made it to the elevator. *All I have to do now is get in and push the button and you know I can do that. Down one floor, out the door, and we begin.* The door opened and I saw the shining floors of the gym area. The room held numerous matted low tables on which patients could do their workouts. The tables were equipped with parallel bars, weight sets, and many other contraptions designed to build strong and healthy bodies. All the staff wore light blue shirts and dark army green heavy canvas belts around their waists, for what I didn't know, but I was sure the belts were not for holding up their pants. As I exited the elevator, one of my staff nurses spotted me and called out, "Hey, great you finally made it. We're so glad you're here." My heart surged with her praise and the elation of my great accomplishments. Then she added, "Real sorry to tell you this, but your hour was up some time ago. See you tomorrow." She turned back to her business at hand.

Well I'll be dipped in a barrel of... you got to be kidding me, come back tomorrow! Man, you want to talk about harsh reality. This has to be wrong. They aren't human, these gentle souls dressed in blue. No they aren't angels either. They are just dressing that way and acting that way to fool me. They are really servants of Fraulein Van Augen sent from the depths of hell to torment me. I faced the elevator and cursed that big silver door as I waited for it to open. *If only I could click my heels and be back in my room.* Wake up, Rich, you know this isn't Kansas.

For the next few days I continued to try to clear the green mile in record–breaking time, only to fall short of my goal. At least I was getting there in under an hour. I continued to push myself, only stopping to rest my horse for a moment and then continuing on to the sacred ground. Each trip I found myself closer and closer to my goal until one day it happened. As I sat breathing hard, I looked around the shiny room and called out, "Hey, I'm here. What's next?" Let me tell you, from that point on nothing was going to stop me or steal away the minutes I was appointed. I was alive and I was moving forward even if it was sometimes at a snail's pace. It didn't much matter to me, time that is, because I was given a new clock set at zero. One thing I had was time, and brother let me tell you, I wasn't going to waste a moment. The first game my physical therapist and I played was, *let's see if you can stand*. Now I knew this was going to be a bust, but I was a good student and would take on any and all challenges no matter how silly they appeared at the time. After all, since I had never been here before, I couldn't know what I could do. As I positioned myself in front of the parallel bars and watched the girls strap braces around my knees. *What do they think? I'm faking not being able to stand?* But many times I would try things just to see what happened. All things were for a reason. As I sat waiting like a racer on the downhill slopes, one of the girls unstrapped the army belt from her waist. *Uh oh, what's this?* I looked around for Fraulein Von Augen thinking maybe she had given the sign and they were going to beat me into standing. Then the girls explained the belts. They were called gait belts, and they were wrapped around my waist creating a handle for the therapists to hold me up or stop me from crashing to the floor. They were something like a safety net for the circus acrobats, and they saved me from many hard floors.

"Okay Richard, we want you to place your hands on the bars and on the count of three pull and we will push you up to a standing position. If at any time you feel like you're going to faint, let us know and we will get you back down okay?" As my hands gripped the rails, I felt no strength or power in my arms, but just like when I squeezed the rubber ball, I believed, and so I pulled. As I was lifted, I heard "How do you feel?"

My vision blurred and with a thick tongue, before the last word came out of her mouth, I said, "I'm fainting." Once again, a split second before darkness came, I heard, "He's out, get him down!" Here we go again. It was starting to become kind of funny. At least I wasn't fainting from pain. Strapped and braced, my body resembled a marionette puppet taking a bow. Upon coming to, I said, "Okay, that was fun. Can we do it again?" The girls chuckled with me and said, "That's enough fun for today. We're going to get you back to your room. Just relax. We'll push you this time." Hey, this was living. What a treat. Before I knew it, I was back in bed. But this was only a rest stop because in Fraulein's world you only slept at night. Lunchtime. Down the green mile to dine. As I entered the dining room, I saw many people just as messed up as me and some even worse, if you can believe that. Some had a device to assist in doing some of the most minor feats like holding a spoon. All items were cartoon size, large handled spoons, and knives with huge open grips, plates with backstops, and suction cups, and always straws for drinks. Now for the able–bodied (AB) friends and family members who visited feeding time was quite a sight. As hard as we tried to perfect the use of these helpful devices, they were as cumbersome as attempting the use of chopsticks. Time and frustration and hunger would take over and without a moment of hesitation or embarrassment, we would nose dive into the plate, and it would be proper etiquette. Hey! When in Rome do as the Romans. Helen Keller had nothing on me. See, this was my world now and *can't* was not an option. So everyday I learned a new way to accomplish an old feat, and I believed; if it's physical, its therapy.

> The Lord maketh poor, and maketh rich: he bringeth low, and lifteth up.
>
> I Samuel 2:7

CLIMB EVERY MOUNTAIN

Each day I gained more and more strength. The green mile shrank and the pain struck less often. My general health seemed to be in good standing and all things were moving in a positive direction. In addition to the grueling physical therapy sessions each day, I participated in occupational therapy where I used the strength I had gained to learn to do the ordinary daily functions that I used to take for granted. Stretching and moving my fingers, hands, and arms was a struggle. Reaching over my head once seemed like an impossible task, but now nothing was impossible in my eyes. To achieve and strengthen these motor skills required, many different exercises were implemented using the silliest tools.

In order to achieve the lift of my arm, I stacked rings on a stick using an old favorite child's toy. To increase dexterity and strength in my hands, I used another child's toy, the one in which the plastic shapes fit in the corresponding holes in the plastic ball, with a twist. The activity was timed and I didn't want to lose. When the clock started, I shoved each object, the star, circle, and square into the same hole. I couldn't understand why they became so upset. I did it faster than anyone else and they were all inside the ball.

Now some exercises were not as funny as playing with toddler toys, like trying to tie my shoe after first trying to put it on. At this time, my hands were still like claws and did not have the strength to even hold a regular spoon. However, with great patience on the part of the staff, and my determination, I succeeded in lacing my shoe with one hand. Thank God this is a feat that I no longer have to do, but if the need arises I can.

Every day I looked forward to each session. I learned how to function a little better and became a little more comfortable with my disability each day, and I did not want to waste a moment of the time I had to work on my physical skills. Psychological therapy, however, was a different story. This one I did not wish to partake in and I didn't. I'll explain why.

I looked back on the night of the accident and realized that God had been at my side that fateful evening. He had told me what had happened to me and that I would be all right. Even though there were many times that I did not look for Him or see Him, He was always holding me in His arms and carrying me until I had the strength to survive in this new and challenging world I had been put into. I thought about how much pain and suffering I had endured and overcome. I know now that I survived because of God's glory. I recalled the look of bewilderment in Dr. Handley's eyes when he first had to tell me that I would never walk again, how I learned the evil of the word "can't," how a rubber ball changed my life, how an angel by the name of Sky walked into my life, and how the pain was taken from my body after prayer. All these experiences profoundly changed my attitude enabling me to believe that I could achieve anything and need not fear the darkness. Yet I still really didn't comprehend God's power and grace. Silly me. This would change as all things do, not always in the most pleasant manner. To get strong was the only thought on my mind. No longer did I think of wine, women or song. Just get strong. To do this I had to keep a positive attitude. This is where the psychological therapy fell short. After attending the first session, I knew I would never go back, nor would I go back to my old ways of thinking.

Upon entering the psychological therapy room, I was confronted by a sight that still lingers in my mind. It was such a sad and depressing vision. In this room was a group of other persons with disabilities ranging from severe to most severe. A short bald man dressed in a poorly fitting, wrinkled brown suit led the session. I looked around and all I saw were frowns of despair. You would have thought I had entered a funeral in progress. As I gazed around the room, I noticed an easel with a paper pad and on this pad in bold hideous letters were the words: Depression, Despair, Fright, Sorrow and Sadness. *What is this?* The bald man asked me to please come in and join the group.

An uneasy feeling crept into me, and for good reason. Apparently I was a little late because the therapist started to explain to me what he had been discussing with the group. He said that it was all right to be depressed and sad and that we should take time and accept these feelings and that it was good that we did this.

"What? Wait a minute," I said. "Excuse me for the interruption, but you're telling me I'm supposed to waste time feeling depressed?"

"Yes," he replied. "It's part of your rehabilitation."

Now I understood all the long faces.

"I don't know about the rest of these people," I said, "but I'm not going to sit around here and waste my time feeling sorry for myself. And unless you have some better information to share with me, I'm leaving."

As I prepared to remove myself from the group and exit the room, this so called therapist exclaimed, "Hey! You can't leave. This is part of your rehab program and you must attend."

With that, I looked at him and said, "Well, this is where you're wrong, Doc. It's not part of my rehab program, so you and the rest of this group can waste your time but not mine."

"You give me one good reason why you shouldn't have to be part of this group?"

"Doc, I'll give you two good reasons. One, I'm not going to, and two, there is not a thing you can do about it. Got it? Good." Then I left.

After that I think the report on me was he's not nuts, he's just crazy. So be it. With that behind me I returned to my room.

My bed had a hanging handle which I grasped to pull myself up from a lying position. I soon found myself hanging from this handle to do pull–ups, which I did constantly, thinking the more I pulled the stronger I'd be, and the stronger I became the sooner I would leave the hallowed halls of Marionjoy.

Each day I worked hard to get stronger. One of the tasks I needed to master was to be able to transfer into Pegasus on my own. This was not easy so I was given a transfer board. This device was no more than a polished flat thin board that would be positioned under my buttock and extend as a bridge to the wheelchair or bed or toilet, enabling me to slide across without having to lift myself enough to clear the wheels of Pegasus.

As helpful as this device was, it was an annoyance because I had to carry it with me at all times. Now where do you put a three feet by two feet board on your wheelchair so it does not hinder your mobility or look ridiculous? Since I had never known a person with a disability who used a wheelchair, I thought that maybe all those who used a wheelchair and were independent had to have this board with them at all times. After several weeks of having to deal with the board, I asked one of the staff, "Why do I need this board? Do all persons with disabilities carry one of these around like some sort of name tag?"

"Oh no, Richard, you just are not strong enough. If you were, you would be able to clear the distance over the wheels on your own."

After several more weeks of doing pull–ups in my bed and pinching my fingers under the board upon transferring, I thought I just had about enough with this board and decided to do something about it. I told the physical therapist that I no longer was going to use the board.

"You have to use the board. How else will you get to bed?" she replied.

I said, "Well, if I'm unable to do it without the board, then I'll sleep in Pegasus."

"Oh, no," she replied. "That won't happen. You can't do it, yet. You just can't."

Oh! Yeah, there it was again, that lousy word. A word for those who give up or don't even want to try, and with that I grabbed the board and threw it across the room. As it bounced off the wall, she looked at me and saw the determination in my eyes.

"Well, I guess we won't be needing that anymore now will we? So if you're ready, I'll be here to spot you if you want to try. Are you ready?"

"Yes. I was born ready."

A mere four inches, just four inches was all that was stopping me from reaching my goal. At one point it might as well have been four miles, but like a climber scaling Mt. Everest, I was not going to let a mere four inches stop me from reaching the top. I imagined the climbers standing with their hearts racing, weak from fatigue, muscles screaming from lack of oxygen. They position themselves for the final lunge. I stared at the bed. *Lift lift! By the power of God you will lift me. Now go.* Then in one graceful swoop I flopped on the bed like a carp out of water. My hands, outstretched towards the railing on the opposite side, grasped for that last foothold, or in my case, hand-hold. I pulled with everything I had using my forehead, nose, mouth, teeth—everything—to hang on and pull myself into the bed.

As I lay there breathing heavily, totally exhausted from the climb, I stared to the heavens and smiled and thought now I could climb every mountain.

> Our steps are made firm by the Lord, when he delights in our way; though we stumble, we shall not fall headlong, for the Lord holds us by the hand.
>
> Psalm 37:23–24

ONE STEP FORWARD
TWO STEPS BACK

The days were full of hope and each day I felt I had achieved great things. Being able to hold a spoon or extend my arm or merely lift and hold my head high were great achievements, physically and mentally. The ability just to breathe I now saw as a gift. How great God is to give us the will and desire to wake up each morning with a new breath of air, and new opportunities to achieve great things.

As long as life is good, we don't despair or turn away from God's love, but life is not always good. The road is dotted with potholes and obstacles that may cause us to doubt or want to turn away from God. Let me tell you, if you have any sense, you will think twice before letting that happen. I'm not certain, but I would bet that all of us, at some time, no matter how great we become or how strong and powerful we think we are, even the toughest of tough men cry to the Lord when the devil or death is upon them.

One day I woke feeling tired and suffering with a severe headache. Initially, I was not concerned. I thought maybe I had a cold coming on. I was never so wrong. To this day, when this feeling strikes, I know it will surely get worse. After going through my morning routine of washing up, taking my medications, and having my vitals taken, I felt even worse than when I awoke. Apparently the staff nurse also thought I was ill because she suggested I stay in bed this day.

As the day went on I felt worse and worse. I was so tired I couldn't lift my head and I couldn't get warm. My appetite was nonexistent and I had a fever that was climbing. By the end of day, my temperature was over 102 degrees and still rising. *What in the world is happening?*

By evening I had lost control of my body and senses. I was sweating buckets, yet I was freezing cold and shivering uncontrollably. When my parents arrived, I knew my condition was serious. The doctors diagnosed a severe bladder infection and prescribed a treatment of IVs and antibiotics hoping to reduce my fever, which had reached a dangerous level. I didn't know that the brain can tolerate a temperature over 102 degrees for only a couple days. Any longer and the fever can cause serious injury or death. Twenty–four hours had passed and the clock was ticking. At one time I cried out for someone to help me.

"Please give more blankets, I'm freezing. Please." But the horrible truth was that while I felt like I was freezing, in reality I was burning up inside and the last thing I needed was more heat. I remember a young nurse assigned to me, who like an angel sent from heaven, never left my bedside and kept a constant watch over me. To my amazement, she lay next to me on the bed and held me close, pressing her warm body against my shivering one. It was the only thing she could do to alleviate my suffering a tiny bit. In a lucid moment, I asked her, "Am I going to die?" She held me close and reassured me in a comforting voice that I would be fine. Although for the moment, her warmth drove the cold from me and eased my pain, I really didn't believe her. The peace and power that I had felt in the past weeks had deserted me. I was never more afraid.

> Fearfulness and trembling are come upon me, and
> horror hath overwhelmed me.
>
> Psalm 55:5 (KJV)

How long could my body stand this? How long could I? The medications weren't working. In fact, I was getting worse. In the wee hours of the morning the lights in my room came on and a group of nurses walked in. Why? Why more than one?

"Richard! Your temperature has reached 105 degrees. We must cool you down immediately." I gazed with blurred vision as they approached carrying a tub of water, towels, and alcohol. They pulled the sheet from my bed, the little warmth I was allowed, and started to undress me. Even though I wasn't sure what they were going to do, I felt sure that it was not going to be fun in the least, and it wasn't. As always, the nurse explained what was going to happen. As she talked in a soothing tone, the other two stood by my side and took hold of my arms. "Richard, we have ice water with alcohol which will feel even colder to you. Please forgive us for having to do this but we must. We have to get this fever down now. Please try to hang on and be strong. We know this is not going to feel pleasant."

"Oh God, please help me," I exclaimed as they placed icy wet towels upon my naked body. The torture I experienced when that towel touched my burning skin was what I imagine a steer feels when being branded and I brayed like one. I pleaded with them to stop, but I knew they wouldn't.

Have you ever stuck your hand in a cooler full of ice trying to reach the bottle at the bottom and had to pull your hand out empty because of the burning that the ice caused? Well that is the sensation I was experiencing and I was powerless to stop it. I don't know how long this ice bath went on. I do remember at one point I no longer had the strength or will to fight, because I endured long enough for the fever to drop if only for the moment. The nurses dried my body, covered me once again, and praised me for my strength. Then I fell into a restless tormented sleep. *This journey isn't getting better. It's getting worse.* I was going one step forward and two steps back.

> Cast thy burden upon the Lord, and he shall sustain thee; he shall never suffer the righteous to be move.
>
> Psalm 55:22 (KJV)

FRIGHT IN THE NIGHT

Praise God, because the devil comes in the night, and when he arrives, you better be ready. I am amazed when I hear people without any hesitation say they believe in the works of the devil, but not in the powers of God. How can this be? Years ago, a horrifying movie about a young girl possessed by the devil came out (in actuality it was a young boy). It showed the devil performing his frightening deeds entering those who are young or weak at heart or have let him in. Some people who saw that movie believed in the existence of the devil, yet those same people would not acknowledge God. How can they think this way? If there is a devil and let me tell you I've seen him, then there must be a God. I give thanks that there is.

The days of ice baths continued. I was getting weaker and the doctor decided that if I didn't improve soon, I would be transferred to a hospital. The fever was taking its toll. My nights were filled with restless sleep and my days were filled with despair. I no longer felt like I had the strength to fight. My belief in God and his love for me was starting to fade. In fact, I was beginning to get angry.

One afternoon this horrible anger showed its ugly face. One of the resident nuns stopped by my room. Sister Bernadette was her name, I came to find out. I'll never forget what she said and more so what I said to her.

"Richard," she said in a soft voice, "I hear you're having a terrible time lately. Don't be discouraged. God does these things for a reason." Oh man! I lost it. I let my guard against the devil down, and I was going to have to pay for it.

"What! God does this for a reason?" I yelled. "What kind of God are we talking about? Why? Why would He do this to me? Have I been this bad in my young life that I deserve all that has befallen me? What kind of God is this that takes my legs, leaves me wracked with pain and tormented by infectious sores, and now fills me with a disease that fevers me into delirium? You say that God did this for a reason? Well, to hell with you and your God. Get the hell out of my room and don't come back here, I don't need you or your God."

Oh! Please don't ever believe God doesn't exist. God is, and He lives and walks with us at all times, and often carries us when we don't even know we're being carried, like our own parents who love us and wish no harm ever will befall us. Sometimes we have to take a step back to see if their teachings and beliefs endure even when they're not near.

"Richard, you must have the patience of Job. I know you're angry and hurting. I forgive you and God forgives you and someday you will understand what I have said." Sister Bernadette said, in her angelic voice. With that she left.

As I lay there, even hotter than I already was, I thought God? Yeah, sure. "We'll see. We'll see. Man, did I ever. Let me tell you, what I saw I didn't like and will never forget. The fever escalated to a dangerous level through the night, and I was racked with pain. The chills and sweats seemed never ending. I tossed and turned with no hope in sight. The darkness of the room, once my comfort, became my horror.

"Who's there? Who's there? Mom, Dad, is that you? I need help. Hey! Answer me. Who's there?" I cried. At that moment I heard a laugh, and at the same time I felt someone crawling into my bed. *Oh good it's only my dear nurse coming to comfort me.* "Help me. Can I have some water?" I asked. Again the laugh came, but it was not the laugh of a kind, loving soul. No, this was an evil laugh. My hair stood on end and my heart raced and filled with a fear I had never before known. The darkness of the room solidified upon my bed. I knew this was not an angel of mercy here to comfort me. But who was it? I couldn't see past the railings of the bed. The laughter continued, and now whoever was in my room had climbed in bed with me and was sitting on my chest. I could not turn away. I could not move. I screamed at the sight.

"Oh my God. What have I done?" My mind screamed because I knew what I had done and I knew who was with me, and it was not God, and I let him in.

"Help me. Help me. Someone Help me!" No one came. The laughing continued and the pressure on my chest felt the same as when I was a child and my older brother would pin me down in the old *say uncle* position. I could barely breathe. *Why can't anyone hear me?* The laughing continued. I had never before feared the dark. I had never feared anything that I could think of. But I was full of fear now.

"Dear God in heaven, forgive me. Please save me. I need you. I can't live without you! God save me! Please. Help me," I prayed. And with that, the laughing stopped. I took a deep breath. The fear vanished, and then the lights in the room came on. I once again was able to see the many spots in the ceiling tiles that I counted so many times like stars in the night.

"Richard, it's time for your meds. Would you like fresh water?" a nurse said. I looked around the room and saw the nurse standing in the doorway.

"Why! Why didn't you come when I called? Are you deaf? Couldn't you hear me screaming for help? I've been yelling for a half hour. Didn't you hear me pounding on the walls? Why didn't you come? Why?" I cried.

"Richard, what are you talking about? You weren't screaming. You know if you were, we could hear you with no problem. We're only right outside your door.

What are you talking about? Are you okay?" As I lay their trembling, warmth, a renewed power, a renewed faith, a renewed love, a new hope of life came over me. I was filled with an understanding that I will never forget. Now I knew the devil walks this earth and he visited my room. More importantly, though, I knew that God is, because He saved me from the fright in the night.

> I have heard of thee by the hearing of the ear: but now mine eyes seeth thee.
>
> Job 42:5 (KJV)

HOME AGAIN HOME AGAIN JIGGITY JIG

Well! It's about that time again. I made it. All the days of hard work, all the trials and fears that I had overcome were now coming to an end, or at least for the first part of this incredible journey into the unknown. The constant hours of squeezing balls, lifting weights, stretching my muscles, taking ice baths, and such, were coming to an end. The never–ending support of many doctors, nurses, family members, and friends had brought me close to the day when I would be released from Marionjoy. I learned that there was a life after a spinal cord injury. I knew that I could at least survive. I still was far from being independent, but I had a pretty good grasp on how I could endure life as a person with a disability. The friend-ships I shared as a patient of Marionjoy are forever with me. I saw things I had never seen before. I watched many broken bodies and spirits being restored. I saw miraculous feats of power and strength, out of shear will and love, being per-formed each and every day. While I was overcoming a severe disability myself, many other young men and women were recovering from disabilities worse than mine.

One of the greatest loves I saw was between a young man who had suffered a car accident and now was completely paralyzed from the neck down and a young nurse at the center. This man had no motion other than being able to blow into a tube that maneuvered his wheelchair. He was in constant need of care and support, and he was married to a beautiful TAB, temporarily able–bodied, woman. For some time, I questioned this woman's motives. Was this guy rich? Was she nothing more then a gold digger? Was someone paying her to love him? What was this and how could it be? Well, you know what I found out? She just loved him. That's what it was. She loved him. How great the miracle of love is. Wouldn't you agree? It is a miracle that I now also experience.

In the thirty–some years that I have been disabled, I have had the great fortune to have shared many relationships with fine women, none with a physical disability. Some may have been a little crazy, but that's another story. They all cared for me in some way, shape, or form, but the relationships were never long–term, partly due to my disability and as much as I hate to admit it, partly because of my attitude. *Ouch that hurt, but sometimes the truth does.* Over the years I have learned that it takes a big man or woman to admit their wrongs. I also know that if you have the Word of God in you, you will know you have been forgiven and that all things are possible in God's time. However, it takes a special kind of woman to be able to deal with a disabled man, a woman capable of love and compassion far exceeding the norm.

I learned that my disability could not stop me from holding my head high when I entered a room. I also learned not to frown, because I have to face and endure a little more difficulty in my life than others face. The truth is that we all have some sort of disability. If you are confident and positive others will be attracted to you.

I have been given the gift of being loved by a generous, kind, and beautiful woman, and I praise God for her love. When He sends you this love and gives you the chance to share this love with another, you must cherish it, revel in it, and embrace it like no other, for it is truly a gift. Of course there are other kinds of love. The true love of God never falters and is everlasting. The love of your friends and family is also a gift. This love enables you to achieve great things. As the day approached when I was to be released from Marionjoy, I looked back at what I had accomplished through hard work, determination, the love of my friends and family, and many caring staff and patients who passed through and were a big part of my new life. Some of these encounters changed my life forever. I thank God for the power and peace and love that He gave me in my darkest hours making it possible, for me to once again rejoice and sing: *Home again, home again, jiggity, jig.*

> That Christ may dwell in your hearts by faith;
> that ye, being rooted and grounded in love.
>
> Ephesians 3:17

BOYS' NIGHT OUT

I awoke and shook the cobwebs from my head. *I'm going home today. I'm going home.* The room was already bustling with activity. As I forced my eyes to focus, one of my dear nurses said, "Quite a night last night I heard." *Oh yeah, it sure was.* You see the previous night was a celebration and celebrate we did.

Early the prior afternoon, the activity director, a young energetic ladies man, thought it would be a great idea to take the residents out for pizza and soda at a local pub. *Pizza and soda, sure. I like pizza and soda.* He told me to be in the lobby at five o'clock. Unbeknownst to the poor guy, my mind was already racing. We are going to party. Oh yeah! Time to make a few phone calls. First, I need a driver.

Although I owned a car, it had not yet been equipped with hand controls. Having this done was at the top of the priority list because I needed wheels to regain my independence. I immediately called my close friend Saul and asked that he pick me up at five o'clock. It was a go. Next, babes. We couldn't have a proper party without them. I made a couple of calls and arranged for some female friends to meet us for pizza and soda. I then went to visit a couple of my comrades in the center. Tony, a triple amputee, had lost his legs and an arm after falling on a high voltage power line while working as a linesman. As I entered Tony's room, he was practicing putting on his new prosthesis legs and arm. He had only been walking with them for a couple weeks, but that didn't stop him from accepting my offer to ride with me to the pub. Next I went looking for Fast Eddie, or Mandingo, as I lovingly referred to him. At six feet two inches and two hundred twenty pounds he had been a wide receiver for a professional football team until he suffered nerve damage from a ferocious hit. That hit ended his playing career. When I first saw Fast Eddie, he walked into the therapy room, where the rest of us were trying to lift incredible weights like spoons, and plastic rings, and pencils and pens, and pulled all the weights on the pulley. I wondered what the heck he was doing at Marionjoy. I soon found out that the center was a leader in nerve damage and evaluations, and he was just there for testing.

Because of the time and tide, he and Tony and I became close friends. "Hey Fast Eddie, we're going out tonight, meet me in front at five. Be there or be square," I called.

"Copasetic," he replied.

As five o'clock drew near, my excitement and anticipation was building like a volcano in its last stages before eruption. Not only was I going home in the morning, but I was going out tonight. Now you may be thinking, *get a life, it's only pizza and pop*, and in the past I would have thought the same thing, being the player I was. This night, however, I was as excited as if I were going to dine on the Riviera and dance with showgirls at Caesar's Palace. I hadn't ventured out of the hospital into the real world for six months. It had been more than six months since I had seen a bartender or waitress or ordered a cocktail—I mean pop. And man! I couldn't wait.

Five o'clock arrived and we gathered in the lobby waiting for the van. I sprang the news on the activity director that I wouldn't be riding with him or the others in the van, that I had arranged for my friend to drive me, and that we would follow him to the pizza pub.

"What possible harm could come from us driving separately? We'll be right behind you," I said. "Let's go."

He had great reservations about it, but he did not want to make a scene. He had had to plead with the center to let us go on this excursion. So while he knew he shouldn't allow me to ride separately, he relented. He took a head count, and we headed for Alfie's. It felt great to be in a car sailing down the road with the windows open and the wind rushing in. It felt great to be moving faster than I could go in Pegasus. I felt like I was back in the real world, back with my dear friend, back in the fast lane. Fun was going to be had, tonight. As excited as I was, I was also scared beyond belief. I felt kind of strange when we arrived because the reality was that we were a group of disabled individuals from a rehabilitation center out for the first time in a long time and only for a few short hours. In those days, you rarely saw a person with a disability on the street or in a restaurant or store. The world was inaccessible to the disabled. Handicapped parking areas, curb cuts, remote doors, and access to public transportation were nonexistent. Public restrooms weren't even handicap accessible. So you can imagine the looks that a gaggle of gimps endured that night, and for years to come, when we entered a restaurant.

We were shown to an area that could accommodate this barrage of metal and wheels and canes and crutches totally disrupting the entire room. I have never felt more like an item on display as I did that night. The waitress who served us was somewhat uncomfortable, maybe even a little frightened, dealing with us. I look back on how peculiarly others acted toward us because of our disabilities and I am glad things have changed.

As I was preparing to order, the waitress looked at my friend and asked him what I would like as if I were incapable of speaking or hadn't the mental capacity to speak

"I don't know. Ask him," he replied. We only had two hours of leave, so I felt it best to start off with a Chivas Regal, on the rocks, with a twist. And for dinner I would have a Chivas Regal, on the rocks, with a twist. And let's see, for dessert, how about a Chivas Regal, on the rocks, with a twist.

"Thank you. That will be all for now. I'll let you know if I need anything else," I told her. She left to fill my order, never questioning whether I was of legal drinking age, not that it really mattered to me. I was old enough to do what I liked. I ignored the activity director's disapproving looks. What did I care what he thought? What were they going to do, make me stay another day at the center if I was bad?

The short hours were filled with laughter. Man, it had been a long time since I laughed about anything. Smelling the scent of women and seeing their smiles made the evening most enjoyable. After a few cocktails, or pops as I called them, and enough of being stared at like some zoo animal, my inhibitions and embarrassment were masked by playful antics. We waved Tony's leg through the double-sided fireplace horrifying some women much to our amusement. I guess it was lucky for all that the time had arrived for us to return to the ranch. The check for pizza and pop for the entire group was a drop in the bucket compared to the bar tab we ran up. We thanked our bartender and waitress with a generous tip. They in turn thanked us for a memorable evening and to the relief of the activity director, we filed out. Climbing, wiggling, and falling into our respective vehicles, we continued laughing. We were having a great evening and thought it a shame that we had to end it at such an early hour, but we had to be back to the center by eight o'clock. Or did we? I turned and looked at my friend.

"Hey. How about we take a ride to my old place of employment?" I wanted to go where I used to be a player, where I was Mr. Guerra. "It's only a few miles away."

" No," he replied. "We have to get back. I can't."

"Can't? What do you mean, can't? Sure you can. Who's going to stop us? Besides, what's the big deal? We're all grown men and we all leave tomorrow." As we pulled alongside the van at the stoplight, I looked at Tony positioned behind my friend who was driving. "What do you think Tony?"

Tony removed his leg from his thigh again and said, "Man, if you don't turn right I'm going to bang you with this leg upside your head. Got it?"

Laughing, Black Eddie said, "If I were you home–slice, I'd turn right." The activity director stared into our window as he waited for the light to change. We turned to look at him and he pleaded with horror–filled eyes as if he somehow knew. The light turned green, and we smiled and waved, as we turned right. He went straight and I thought I saw a tear come to his eye. For a moment, I felt a twinge of sorrow for him, knowing how helpless he was to change the situation, but the twinge lasted only a moment.

We turned into the parking lot of the Lodge, and my heart raced as I the thought of all those I soon would be meeting again, all those who knew me as Mr. Guerra, all those who would now see me as a totally different person, a person with a disability. Will I be accepted? Will they welcome me? Will they turn in shock and horror or sorrow? Maybe this isn't such a good idea. Maybe I should just accept the fact that I am now disabled and this past life was only a dream and just go back to the center and not put myself and my friends through the embarrassment. Maybe I should just turn back. Nawww! I was past the point of no return. This was the time to prove to myself and the world that I was back in a new and improved form. And so I entered. As the large door of the main lounge swung open, all eyes turned. This was something that I would have to get used to and accept for many years to come. Although the staring of the patrons was unsettling, I was not as concerned about the looks they shot me as the looks that came from the staff that knew me, worked with me, loved me, and had not seen me for many months. Now they saw me in a wheelchair. All in one moment, the look of shock, surprise, and sadness flashed in their faces, and then joy settled in their eyes. They looked at me as if I were a celebrity. The bartenders came from behind the bar and the waitresses came from the tables where they were taking orders to get close to me. They hugged me and kissed me and congratulated me and welcomed me back, and tears flowed down my cheeks because I knew that I had made it back, and I thanked God for the boys' night out.

> O keep my soul, and deliver me: let me not be ashamed; for I put my trust in thee.
>
> Psalms 25:20 (KJV)

THE WORLD'S NOT FLAT

I signed the last papers, said my last goodbyes, and with great joy, finally left for home! I no longer had to live at the center. I no longer had to sleep in a hospital bed. I no longer would be surrounded by white walls and fluorescent lights. I no longer would count holes in the tiled ceiling. Oh the joy and the thrill. Oh the love. I had not spent a night in my mother's house for years by choice, but now I couldn't wait to return to the warmth and safety of the home that I spent so many years growing up in with my brother and sisters. The thought of enjoying a home cooked meal prepared only like my mother could, was far beyond bliss. Even though I had lived and survived as a grown man in the world at the age of eighteen, I now felt like a newborn child. All the old was now new. There were going to be challenges that I would face that I never could imagine. There would be doubts and fears that I would have to overcome. Would the square peg that I had become, fit into the round world?

On the return trip home, as I passed many familiar places, I thought of the past and sorrow filled my heart.

I remembered these places and the times as if I were an old man reminiscing about his youth. I looked at the trees and thought of the many hours I spent climbing to the tops and swaying in the wind as a youngster. I thought of the fields that I lay in, watching the clouds go by. Missing the past is a sorrow that we all face in our lives. It is not always a good feeling, but it is a feeling, nevertheless, that we must endure. To survive we must endure this loss with a never–ending faith in God's purpose and direction that He has had for us since we were born. This faith is what brought me home again.

My heart raced as we turned the corner and proceeded up the street toward my home. Incredible feelings flowed through me. The house itself seemed to welcome me home. With a toot of the horn, family members flowed out the door like a river of love to greet me. As I swam through the hugs and kisses and tears and smiles and entered the door, I smelled the aromas of my childhood and I saw my dear mother's smile. She opened her arms wide to receive me. At that moment I felt nothing but power and peace, love, and joy, and I thanked God I was home.

This first day home was the beginning of a new and challenging journey. Unlike Marionjoy where floors were flat and smooth and doors opened wide, where handles were big and light switches low, I would now have to adapt to the world outside the center. The outside world was not equipped for nor cared about the needs of the disabled. This world would not change for years to come.

The home that I grew up in was a modest three–bedroom home. The front door faced a small bedroom. To the right of the front door was a long hallway that led to the kitchen. Off the hall on the right was a bathroom and on the left an entrance to the living room. At the back of the living room were two small bedrooms, one in each corner. On the left side of the kitchen corner was the back door that led to the yard where, for so many years, I climbed to the top of the large oak tree, which supported my many tree houses. It also held strong the large rope which all of us swung on for endless hours on warm summer days. These times I remember, to this day. Although the house was small, Mom's love always made it a welcoming home. While I was hospitalized, my family had worked at adapting the house enough to accommodate me comfortably. Mom gave up the first room in order for me to have easy access to the bathroom. This was made possible by the work of my dear brother–in–law, Tom, and others opening up a wall to the bathroom. Since the house was built on a slab, there was not much more that had to be done in order for me to be able to continue on my road to independence.

Whenever the family gathers, we spend most of our time in the kitchen. I guess food brings people together. We enjoy scrumptious meals and countless hours of card playing at the dining table. We even put a couch in the kitchen for those who needed to rest and unbuckle their pants after a hearty meal. It was a comfortable home, but small, so plans were made to build an addition.

After many months, through the love and hard work of my sister and her husband, the two–story addition was completed. Ten stairs led from the kitchen up to two new rooms and a bath. Three steps down from one of those rooms was a recreation room complete with a fireplace and a small bedroom. Now this was a beautiful addition to the house, but it wasn't really accessible for me. Or was it?

I was able to maneuver throughout the first floor of the house without too much difficulty. However, going downstairs or upstairs, as I'm sure you guessed, was not possible. Therefore, my brother–in–law devised a ramp to the recreation room. The normal ratio for a ramp is one step to three feet, but in this case, there were only seven feet for three steps, so the angle of this ramp was somewhat frightening to say the least. The only way up or down was with assistance and even then it was some-times a scary and hairy ride. There was not much room for error. The recreation room became one of my favorite spots, because it had the stereo system, my conga drums, which I had become quite good at playing because of the countless hours I had to practice, and it was large and roomy.

As I became more comfortable and sure of myself in my surroundings, I could spend a couple of hours a day at home alone. In the morning, my sister would assist me down the ramp and set me up with snacks and drinks enough to sustain me for the three hours she would be gone to work. I was always secure knowing that with one phone call a neighbor, friend, or family member would be at my side if the need arose. This confidence allowed other family members to perform their daily routines of going to work, to the store, and on other outings without fearing that I was in danger.

Each day after my sister Margo left, I would stare at that ramp and think how far I still was from being independent. The ramp seemed to taunt me, laughing at me, saying, "See, you're disabled and you have to stay right where you're at. You couldn't leave even if you wanted to. You can't. You can't. You can't!" Well you can guess what happened. Each day I faced that ramp. *Somehow, someway, I have to get up this ramp. I have to.* Now I knew that this was not going to be an easy task and possibly even an impossible task. The angle of this ramp was so extreme that I would have to position my body so that my chest was against my knees and keep it that way the entire climb and have the strength to roll myself up the slope. To this day, no able–bodied man with the ability to balance and catch himself if he started to fall has ever achieved rolling up the ramp. I, however, had to beat this ramp. It was as though reaching the top would be my initiation into the world of independence. I would succeed or spend the rest of my days at the bottom always looking up wondering what it would feel like to be at the top.

So the battle began, man against ramp, mano a mano, no assistance in any form, just Pegasus and me. There was no margin for error. One slip and I would pay a price, lumps and bumps. Each day after my sister left and I heard the door close, I would position myself in front of the ramp staring up. I didn't want anyone to know what I was going to attempt, for I'm sure they, as sane people, would have tried to stop me. I would roll forward so the front wheels rose to the incline. I learned the hard way if I attempted to push at this point in an upright position, I would tip over backwards and experience the agony of defeat and be rewarded with a lump. I had the lumps to prove it. With my chest against my knees and my hands gripping the wheels with a death grip, I pushed forward and upward, and I moved. The problem that arose immediately was that I had no way to continue with a second push. Once my push extended my arms to the bottom of the wheel I would have to let go to grab the top of the wheel in a split second or succumb to gravity and lose any meager ground I had gained. I would have to be faster and stronger than gravity and combat the fear of slipping back and facing the crash and burn. What I found is that I could not push in the normal manner. I would have to push in increments of five to six inches keeping my grip always at the top of the wheel.

Each day as I faced this challenge, I had to overcome the physical obstacles and the even more challenging, the mental obstacles. You see, the more times I attempted this feat, the harder it became. As I achieved one rotation length of the small front wheel upward, the next rotation required even more strength, balance, and determination. You might think that after banging my head enough times on the ground I would start to wonder if all the pain was worth the gain. After all, if I just waited someone would help me up. *I'm disabled. No one expects me to perform these feats. There's no reason for me to. It can't be done.* But there it was again, that nasty word, "can't." So every day I pushed and every day I rolled back. After one or two attempts I would be totally exhausted having only made a few inches of progress.

Every day that I made progress however, I closed in on my goal. Every day I rolled a few more inches upward, and every day I grew stronger and more determined. Every day I believed, every day. As in all things, if you believe and don't fear or regret the little setbacks that occur, if you believe in the powers that God has blessed you with, you will succeed. This I know to be true because one afternoon after weeks and weeks of trying, I succeeded. Much to my sister's amazement, I greeted her at the front door. As I hugged and kissed her, I realized that in my new world I would have to work harder than I had ever worked before and believe in the love and power that God gives us, because the world is not flat.

> With you I can rush an armed band, with my
> God to help I can leap a wall.
>
> Psalm 18:29 (KJV)

UP AND DOWN, DOWN AND UP

My dear readers, this chapter is dedicated to all the mothers of the world who love and care for their children to the end of time, and to all the men who think that it is an easy task to raise these gifts from God.

The strength that I had gained and was gaining each and every day was a true blessing. The numerous attempts at the ramp and the successes proved this to be so. The more times I succeeded the more confidence I had that I could face and overcome any challenge set before me, no matter how big. I would soon learn, however, that it is not always the big challenges that I face that teach me the most. Sometimes the littlest of giants have stopped me in my tracks and dropped me to my knees.

A few months after I returned home, my sister Margo gave birth to my precious niece, Vesta, a true gift and angel of God. The joy that she brought to me, the family, and the house, outweighed all of the suffering and pain I had endured. Praise God for this life. Holding her in my arms for the first time is a feeling I will never forget. This beautiful little ten–pound baby girl, now a mother herself, looked up at me and smiled as I kissed her gently and whispered to her, "Hello. I'm your Uncle Richard and I love you very much."

Close your eyes with me and inhale and you will smell that wonderful scent that only comes from a freshly bathed, powdered, and diapered infant. What joy she brought to me. Even in my limited physical condition, I knew that I would do anything for her if asked. And that day came.

For the next few months, my days consisted of believing, working at becoming stronger, and enjoying life in the real world. I spent many hours outside enjoying the warmth of the sun and the healing powers it seemed to have. I often shared lunch outings with friends and went on shopping trips. These events challenged me in new ways.

One day my sister Margo asked me, "Bro, do you think you could watch and care for the baby for the morning hours while I go to work?" Now up to this point for the last five or six months since the baby's arrival, my interaction was mostly looking at her in the crib or holding her for a short time until my arm went numb from her weight. A few times I actually fed and burped her. My sister worked only blocks away and would only be gone from eight o'clock until noon, a mere four hours. I mean come on, how hard could it be to watch this bundle of joy? After all the challenges that I had faced and overcome there wasn't even the slightest doubt in my mind. I could fulfill this request. It would be a cake walk, easy as pie. No sweat. So I said yes.

"Are you sure?" she asked.

"Hey, just let Uncle know what has to be done and I'll cover it."

With that she ran down the list of tasks. Simple, I thought, the baby wakes about nine o'clock. If she cries, check to see if she needs to be changed. If not, she probably needs a bottle. Feed her and burp her. She's a happy baby so what could possibly go wrong? I sent my sister on her way, then I kept vigil over my niece.

Shortly, I heard the gurgling of the waking princess. I rolled to the basinet where she had been sleeping. She looked up at me with a smile of delight to be awake. The fun was about to begin.

The first step was to lift her from the crib to my lap. I didn't think about lacking the balance just to grab and lift her, but as I attempted to pick her up, I could see that both of us would land on the floor if I wasn't careful. I wasn't about to let this happen. As I looked over the situation, I decided the best way to pick her up would be to mimic a mother cat carrying her kitten. No, I didn't place her in my mouth, but close. I grasped her garment securely from the front and lifted her like a crane and set her on my lap. It worked just fine. This was the first time I had ever lifted her myself and I was proud of my accomplishment. We sat for a moment smiling at each other until she'd had enough and told me so in a high-pitched cry that would have curled my toes, if they were capable of curling. For a brief moment I felt a touch of panic and wanted to cry with her, but this desire passed and uncle came into play. Okay! I thought, let's check her out. I knew she was not in any pain, so next I checked her diaper to see if it was wet. Holding her close to my chest, I reached into her diaper. Well! It didn't take a brain surgeon to know that it was changing time. If the smell that suddenly drifted to my nose gagging me and bringing tears to my eyes didn't tell me, definitely the mass of warm green slime that appeared on my hand as I pulled it from the diaper did.

Let me tell you, in my life I have smelled dead skunks, rotten chicken, and spoiled milk, but nothing, and I mean nothing, prepared me for what I smelled now. It took all my will power not to hurl on her head. How could anything so small and so beautiful excrete such a hideous, gut-wrenching, vile scent? Not even the result of beans, sauerkraut, and egg sandwiches ingested with too much beer could compare. After I composed myself, I rolled toward the couch to lie her down in order to change her and let me assure you, I did this as quickly as I could.

Once I cleaned her and sprayed the room with enough deodorizer that I could at least continue without blurred vision, I prepared to put the clean diaper on her. Now if you recall, in these days there were no easy-stick tabs or Huggies. These were the days of the old-fashioned cloth diaper with the oversized safety pins. I crane-lifted her and placed her on the diaper which I wasn't quite sure how to fold. I thought of how diapers had looked on the Flintstones, shaped like a V, but it just didn't look right, so I repositioned the diaper for the square–folded look. Folding the diaper was the easy part. I hovered over her and prepared to fasten the pins. After numerous attempts and several pricks of my fingers I realized I did not have the finger dexterity to close and secure the pins. So now what? She was growing ever more impatient with my incompetence and I did not want to be subjected to that ear–piercing wail that was sure to come if I did not hurry. Opting for the only solution I could think of, I wrapped her in a big towel. Yeah man, that worked great, and I really think she liked it more than those stupid confining diapers. The towel was roomy. That was the ticket. Life was good again. All was peaceful at the ranch. I placed her in her little walker to catch my breath and then the phone rang.

I answered and a salesman was on the other end trying to pitch some item that I did not need. Then the most horrifying thing happened, at least horrifying to me at the time. The baby rolled toward the throw rug and flipped over backwards in her walker. Without hesitation I lunged for her forgetting that my legs would not catch me. I smashed face–first onto the floor. My eyes watered profusely and blood poured from my nose, but I reached her, up righted her, and comforted her, all in one motion. Meanwhile, the voice on the phone called, "Hello. Hello, is anybody there?" I checked the little princess over to make sure she was crying in annoyance and not pain and then dragged myself to the phone and hung it up. In spite of all my efforts however, her siren came, an endless wailing, and all the *goo–goo's* and *ga–ga's* were not going to please her. Finally, I figured out the princess wanted food and food she would have. I went to the kitchen to warm her bottle of milk.

It was 1978—these were the days before microwave ovens, so I had to warm the bottle in a pan of water on the stove. After I prepared the bottle and placed the pan on a low flame to warm, the phone rang again. This time it was my father just calling to see how things were going. Not wanting to worry him, I said all was well, and just at that moment the unthinkable happened, again. The baby flipped over on another rug in the kitchen causing me to perform the death–defying leap onto my face again. Yeah, maybe lightning doesn't strike twice in the same place, but my nose sure did. Here I was again, comforting the baby from a prone position while a voice on the phone called, "Hello, Hello, is everything all right?" As if this wasn't enough excitement, the milk had not only warmed but was burning on the stove. I grabbed the phone, said I had to go and threw it towards the hook on the wall to hang it up.

After righting both of us again and calming the princess, I prepared a new bottle of milk and fed her. As she nestled in my arm and enjoyed her meal, her eyes took on a far–away look, and she smiled with relief. Actually, she smiled with relieving, I soon discovered. For at that moment, the unmistakable odor of poo–poo wafted up to my nose and the towel exploded with a lava–like flow of green slime. All I could do was hold her as she gurgled with delight and I gagged with repulsion. Now, I don't remember dialing, or even hearing the phone ring, but I remember saying, "Sis, please come home. Please, come home now." Then I waited.

A few moments later, like a distant sound I heard the door open. My sister stared at me, stunned at first by my blood–crusted nose and green slime shirt. Then, when she saw her baby sleeping peacefully in my arms and assured herself that I was okay, amusement danced in her eyes and she attempted to smother her laughter. I looked back at her through battle–worn eyes and muttered in some strange language what had transpired since she left. "Please, don't ever let me attempt this again," I said. With this she snatched the darling from my lap and helped me to the shower. The game was over for me. Did anyone get the license plate of that truck?

To this day, I give all the credit to all the moms who deal with these struggles every day with smiles on their faces. Conquering the ramp was nothing compared to caring for an infant. However, the strength I had built rolling the ramp enabled me to upright myself whenever the need arose. Caring for my princess niece, I realized how much I loved her and how much I loved life. I never really minded cleaning up the mess, hitting the floor or getting up and down, down and up.

> As this my body is racked with pain, pang seize
> me, like those of woman in labor; I am staggered
> by what I hear, I am bewildered by what I see.
> Isaiah 21:3 (KJV)

READY WILLING AND DISABLED

In an ever–changing world it is good to live in the land of the free and the brave, to share inalienable rights, and to live where all are created equally, all except persons with disabilities that is.

It had been over a year since my accident, and I had continued to gain strength and even had some more return of my motor functions. In fact, more of my motor functions returned than is normal with such a severe break and nerve damage. For this I thanked God and hard work too.

I continued to spend many days going on outings with my friends. As a result, I started to realize how uninformed the world was about people with disabilities. Having spent the majority of my time since the accident in either a hospital or rehabilitation center or among those who loved me dearly, I was not really aware of the obstacles that awaited me in the real world. Nor was I aware of the stares that I would be subjected to. The world was designed for able–bodied people and the disabled were expected to remain hidden in their homes

Countless times, when I was seated in a restaurant with an able–bodied person, the waiter or waitress looked past me and asked my companion what I would like to order as if having a physical disability left me also without the capability of making decisions. Waiters and waitresses who did speak to me tended to get real close or bow down toward me as if I were hard of hearing. This treatment was most degrading when I was in the company of a woman. I felt the greatest heartbreak, though, when the whispers of sorrow or sympathy flowed through a room, when people looked at me and then quickly turned away and when the arms of inquisitive children tugged on their mothers who tried to shield them from having to look at my disability. I had to come to terms with all of these things along with the lack of accessibility. I had taken accessibility for granted in my able–bodied days, but now it was an issue that I would have to address not only for my own well being, but also for the minority of persons with disabilities. And so the battle began.

How could I help to change these misguided, misinformed views many people held about the disabled? Despite whether anyone would listen or care, I knew that I needed to try to change the attitudes of the general population in order to live with dignity and respect. As I thought about how I was going to achieve this change, I realized I first had to look into myself and see how I saw myself as a person with a disability and how I reacted to those with disabilities prior to my accident. Then, and only then, could I address the misperceptions about those disabled.

Thinking back, I realized that I had seen a person who used a wheelchair only once when I was in high school. Then I was one of those who stared and gawked at this disabled boy. In our school the elevator was only for the disabled. We all joked about buying an elevator key. Now I find that a disability is not a joking matter, nor should it have been then, but it was. Now I was he, but without the key.

At first I was uncomfortable and embarrassed when I went out, as if I didn't belong in public. Always upon entering a room I was the object of attention, yet people would go out of their way to avoid contact with me as if I were the plague. I found it very difficult to use public restrooms because I had to use a device to assist in my relieving myself and I dreaded enduring the stares of fellow relievers. Of course, sometimes I couldn't use public restrooms because they were inaccessible. I also resented being treated like a second–class citizen, being talked over as if I wasn't there or able to respond. They now ignored me, Mr. Guerra, who ran restaurants and was respected by waiters, waitresses, hosts, and hostesses. I became angry, not so much at uninformed people, but at myself, for acting like I was disabled and looking the part. Why should I expect anyone to treat me any differently than I viewed myself? Do you remember the old verse: "If it looks like a duck and walks like a duck?" Well, there you have it. I hit it on the nose. If I looked like a gimp and acted like a gimp, I must be a gimp. Right? Wrong! No more. Was I going to be embarrassed of who I was. I had fought and overcome too much to allow myself to be treated or to act in such a manner ever again. Like the raven, I said, "Nevermore." From this moment on, I would carry myself and hold myself upright with pride, dignity, and honor.

To combat the bowing of individuals as they spoke to me I sat up as straight as possible and even leaned back a little. It worked. This posture made those who spoke with me stand up. Next, I had to figure out how to combat unwarranted apologies. When going through a crowded room I often had to make people aware that I was behind them, and like everyone else, I would say "Excuse me!" Inevitably, people would reply, "Oh, I'm sorry," and then allow me to pass. I didn't think about the apologies at first, but the more I received, the more I began to wonder if others received apologies in similar situations. So I questioned a couple of friends.

"Hey, when you need to get past someone in a room, what do you say?" I asked.

"I say excuse me, wait for them to move, and then proceed," they said.

"Okay. What if someone asks you to excuse him or her so they can get by? What do you say?"

"Well, nothing really. We just move or say, 'sure, no problem,'" they replied.

Just as I suspected. For some reason, when I asked to be excused, people always apologized for being in my way. Although this was nice of them, I didn't feel I deserved an apology. So to help change this behavior, I began responding, "No need to apologize and thank you." I hoped this made others feel like there was no reason to treat me differently in this common everyday situation, and it seemed to work.

The next time that I was treated with disrespect in a restaurant, I addressed the problem directly, but politely. I didn't want to alienate or offend others just because they lacked awareness about the disabled. What I hoped to affect was a way of thinking. I was dining out with a lady friend one evening and the host ignored me. I said to the host, "Excuse me. May I ask you a question?" "Sure," he replied.

"When a man and a woman are waiting to be seated, by etiquette do you address the man or the woman of the party."

"Well, the gentleman by all means."

"That's correct," I said, being versed in the art of serving. "So why are you not asking me as the gentleman of this party? Being in a wheelchair should not deprive me of the respect that I should be given. Wouldn't you agree?"

The host was dumbfounded. He knew that he had been wrong in his actions and he apologized. I knew he had learned a lesson as had others who were within hearing distance. As we were led to our table, I felt a surge in my being, knowing that I had stood up for my rights and the dignity of all of us with disabilities. My partner was proud of me too, and I knew this was the beginning of an education process for the masses. I was ready, willing, and disabled.

> In everything set them an example by doing what is good. In your teaching show integrity, seriousness and soundness in speech that cannot be condemned.
>
> Titus 2:7–8 (KJV)

LESSONS

It seemed that each day I was confronted by a new situation, a new challenge, and a new lesson. In these challenges, I found myself sometimes questioning my faith. However, because of these trials set before me, I now at forty–eight years of age, at this writing, I accept and truly realize the power and glory of our God and have achieved a peace and power that sustain me. I am also able to share this with others and will continue to do so in the name of God. I only wish that I would have stayed focused on the Word at a younger age, after all the blessings God has bestowed upon me throughout my life. The reality, however, is that I didn't stay focused, so then I have to ask myself, why? Why? How many times does God have to prove His love for me, for all of us, before we will believe and continue to believe? Of course many have realized this truth and even though they face hard times and difficult challenges, they do so with faith, believing in God's plan, and purpose. Like our Savior Jesus Christ, they fear not. Now I look back and am amazed that I survived, and I give thanks to God for my life each and every day.

I had been learning the ropes for more than two years. I was fortunate to have strong, loving, family members and friends. They enabled me to be independent because I knew that someone was always close by to give me a hand if I failed at the first or second or even third attempt at a new task. Strangely, as often as I was out in public, I never saw another person with a disability, not in the stores, not in the restaurants, not in the clubs. There had been so many at the rehab center, yet once I left there I never saw another person in a wheelchair in public. Where were they? They were at home, for a couple reasons. They lacked accessibility and they lacked discretionary income. Few persons with disabilities could afford to go out for nights on the town and those who could afford it needed transportation. At that time, public transportation was not accessible. Man! There weren't even ramps, which we take for granted nowadays.

Finally, one day upon entering one of my favorite watering holes, a place that I was familiar with and comfortable in, much to my great surprise I happened upon another man riding a steel horse. We caught each other's eyes and exchanged a knowing look. As we greeted one another, I knew what mountain men must have felt when they crossed paths after blazing trails on their own for years. Even though they were strangers, upon meeting, they were brothers in kind. We talked about our present lives as persons with disabilities. We shared stories of how we came to this time in our lives and we both realized that we were living in an inaccessible world. If we were going to survive and be contributing members of the work force and society, we would need to change some attitudes. Those who saw us as drains on the welfare and social security systems needed to be educated. With a need to hope for a better future, we vowed to change our own attitudes and those of society at large.

My friend and I talked for many hours and probably drank more than we should have, something I no longer do. Praise God.

It was as if we were the only two people on the planet who understood each other and we would soon have to go our own ways, never to meet again. When we parted company, I experienced a dreadful loneliness and a sad realization that maybe things weren't as good as I thought they were. I was going to suffer another two years of feeling this way. Eventually, hope would return and an opportunity to help change our country to make it a better place to live for the largest minority of the time, people with disabilities, would present itself. In the meantime, I had to continue to learn my own lessons and these were not always easy, but I knew I had to press on, no matter how frightened I was.

For two years, I had the security of knowing someone was always close by and my room was safe in a somewhat accessible way. However, I knew if I stayed in my comfort zone, I would never truly achieve independence. The time had come to venture out on my own. This simple venture, however, was one of the most frightening challenges I would face. It was not so much the physical aspect of this challenge that was frightening, but the mental anxiety that it caused. Even though I had gone out many times to many different places, I realized I had never done this alone, just me and Pegasus, a man and his horse. No one else would be along to divert the attention and stares that I was certain to draw. All day long I wrestled with the notion of going out to a nightclub by myself. Although I was scared, I knew I was going to do it. This was just another battle that I was preparing for and like anyone going into battle I experienced a sense of anticipation and cold fear.

Of all the lessons I learned, one of the most important was not to lie to myself. I know when I'm trying to fool myself, and even more importantly, God knows. It's better to be able to look at myself in the mirror and question my own actions and even admit to myself how afraid I am of a situation than to lie to myself. Besides, if I lie to myself then I am lying to God because He sees me, is with me and is in me at all times just as He was with Adam and Eve in the beginning. They tried to hide from Him in the Garden of Eden, but He knew, and they were shamed. So why shame myself? There is no need. God will be with me, and with you at all times. He carries us when we are weak. He guides us when we are lost. He gives us the strength we need when we are afraid. With His help, we shall overcome any and all obstacles. So with this knowledge I prepared. I wore a tightly creased shirt and slacks and a highly polished spit–shined pair of shoes. I left, alone, in the night to see what I could see, to be what I could be, and that was me.

I was now able to drive, thanks to one of the first accommodating inventions on the market besides wheel-chairs, hand controls for vehicles. Pushing down on a rod that extended from the left side of the steering column depressed the gas pedal, and pushing the rod forward depressed the brake pedal. With a little practice and a few scares, none serious, I was once again able to obtain a license to drive, which helped me to regain some of my independence.

I parked the car at an angle in the lined parking space. You see, in these days there were no handicap–designated areas, so if I did not park in this manner and a car parked next to me, I wouldn't be able to open my door wide enough to let Pegasus out. This was a lesson I learned after waiting in a snowstorm for someone to move their car. For a moment I waited, contemplating the test I was putting myself through. I had patronized this club many times in the past, so I knew there was a slight curb, nothing I couldn't handle. I had learned to pop wheelies in order to jump curbs and had plenty of knots on my head from the first failed attempts. As years go by, I find my desire to pop wheelies waning. If you have ever sat on a chair, reclined balancing on the two back legs, and then suddenly felt that drop in your stomach when the chair is about crash to the floor, but at that very second caught yourself, you know how popping wheelies felt to me. As I age, I guess I just don't like that feeling any more. Anyway, I sat in the car thinking once I made it up the curb, I could get in the door and I would be in the nightclub.

This club had a unique sunken bar, so the bartender was lower than the patrons. The bar stools were table level instead of the usual high stools which was great for me because everyone else would be sitting level with Pegasus and me. *Just be cool, man. This is what you have trained for, what all the lessons have been for. You're good at this. In fact, you're one of the best. Go man. Just do it.*

And I did. As the door swung open, I felt the rush of air passing by me, and in an instant all the lessons of the past years flashed before me: all of the pain and anguish, all the despair and hope, all the physical accomplishments that I had achieved in the past years, all the frights in my mind that I continue to battle, all the lessons that I had been taught and those I taught myself seemed to rush through me as fast as air rushed by me. I felt as if I had not moved for quite some time, but as my eyes focused on the room and I gazed into the colored lights of the room and heard the music, I knew that only a moment had passed. As I entered, I felt an overwhelming sense of peace and power that I had never felt before. I know now it was the grace of God that enabled me to go forward. With my head held high and a smile on my face I rolled towards the bar. The bartender greeted me with a nod and a smile like I was an old friend. "Hi Rich, how are you? Where are your buddies?"

"Well, I'm just hanging out by myself tonight, just wanted to hear some tunes and see some smiling faces," I answered. After placing my order, I turned toward the crowd and gazed at all the faces that seemed to be watching me. And they were. I smiled and nodded, holding back my fear of embarrassment, a fear that is one of the biggest of all men and women and a fear I have not experienced for many years. I turned back toward the bar as if this was just another night out and a common occurrence. Then I knew all would be right from then on.

"Hey, this one's on me, you're cool," the bartender said, with a wink and a smile.

Through the night I shared in many conversations and made new friends. As I sat there sipping my drink, I took a moment to reflect on the evening's events. My heart swelled knowing that I had done it. I had done it because I believed in myself and was blessed with God's Lessons.

> Every word of God is flawless; he is a shield to those that take refuge in him."
>
> Proverbs 30:5 (KJV)

ANOTHER CHANCE

Throughout our lives, without our knowing, God is leading us, guiding us, giving us another chance. Even when we turn our backs on Him, He gives us that chance. We often try to sway from God's grace thinking that we are in control and that we have all the answers. Many times in my life I tried to make my own way down the path only to find myself alone and in the dark. Every time I found myself face down again, I cried out to my Lord to save me, help me, give me just one more chance. And you know what? He always did, He always does, and He always will. This I believe to be true. After reading this chapter you may find it to be true too. Of course you have the choice to believe or not believe I pray to God that you choose to believe, just as I have.

It had been almost three years since I was released from Marionjoy. I spent most of my time trying to adapt and overcome all the challenges that were set before me, and continuing to gain strength, both physically and mentally. Although I had gained physical and mental strength, I was lacking in one most important area, believing and following the Word of God. Now you may ask yourself, "why?" I surely did. After receiving so many chances, how could I have the gall, nerve, or audacity to forget the gifts that God had given me. To forget that it was He who gave me hope and carried me when I was weak. It was He who took away the pain and gave me the power to believe all things are possible. It was He who brought me back from the grasp of death and gave me life more than once. Yet in those days I forgot or perhaps I was just too selfish to give my love back to Him. I know the latter to be true. Once again I can only praise God and thank Him for his love and for never forsaking me in the times I did not thank Him.

On a warm summer morning I awakened from a restless sleep, weak, fevered, scared, and panting like a dog. When my temperature was high, I tended to breathe in this manner because my body was trying in its own way to reduce the heat that was building inside me. For a week I had felt tired and for the past couple of days, experienced pain and a fever throughout my body, yet I couldn't pinpoint the cause. What I did know was that I was dying. With my last ounce of strength I called out to my sister Becky to come quickly.

She entered the room and I gasped, "Help me. We have to go to the hospital. I think I'm dying." Now, as I look back to that time, I realize she must have also known somehow, someway, although I had no visible signs.

"Okay, Bro. We're going now," she said as she held me close. She immediately lifted me out of bed, plopped me into Pegasus and rushed me to the car. As we sped to the hospital, I felt my dear sister's hand gripping my arm and heard her calmly telling me, "Stay awake, Bro. Please don't go to sleep. Stay awake, we'll be there soon."

The warm sun streamed through the window and warmed my cheek, yet I felt chilled, tired, and weak. The five–mile route to the hospital was familiar to me and through blurred eyes I could see where we were and knew the clock was ticking. *Hurry, Sis. Please hurry. I don't feel very well.* No, I didn't feel well at all and teetered on the brink of unconsciousness. Still, as if from far away, I heard her voice calling to me to stay with her. *Okay, I will but you have to hurry.*

By the time we arrived at the hospital, I was slipping over the brink. As the car door opened, I lifted my head one last time and saw doctors and nurses adorned in white jackets running toward me. They lifted me onto a stretcher and rushed me inside. All the time my sister kept saying, "Stay with us, Richard. Don't leave me. I love you. Stay with me. We are here. You will be okay." I drifted in and out of consciousness. I felt the coolness of the hall and saw the overhead lights flashing by as I was whisked into the surgery room. As strange as it might seem, I always felt reassured when I saw those oversized lights hanging over me like a man–made sun, and heard the controlled chaos that was part of an emergency room.

For the third time I was facing death. Was this the third strike in my game of life? Or was it a ball? No one was on base. The doctors asked questions and I tried to communicate to no avail. It was time to hit the showers. Hey coach, can I sit out the rest of the game? I think I'm done now. But there it was again, that loving feeling, that power and strength. Peace flowed through my body, the reassurance that all would be fine. Sleep now, I am with you. And I smiled. As I closed my eyes, I took a deep breath, not knowing if I would awake from this sleep nor caring.

When I awoke from surgery, my mind screamed: "Give me air, give me air!" I grabbed for the mask as it came toward my face. As I breathed, I cried. Why I don't know, but I did.

"It's okay, Richard. Do you know where you are?" someone asked. "You gave us quite a scare. We almost lost you," the doctor said. "But you'll be okay now." He must have read my puzzled expression. "We didn't know at first what was wrong. Your white blood cell count was very high. You were being poisoned inside, but you couldn't feel it. You didn't know that your appendix had ruptured and was killing you slowly for the last couple of days. It's a wonder that you're here. Rest now everything is fine." How right he was. Praise God. How great life is. Let me tell you, my life changed again. I had been given another chance. What would I do with it? Would I squander it? Or would I cherish it? Only time would tell. I praise God that He gave me a choice. Another chance.

This is what the Lord says: As I have brought all this great calamity on this people, so I will give them all the prosperity I have promised them.

Jeremiah 32:42 (KJV)

TIME TO TRY, TIME TO FLY

The first four years after the accident, I was in and out of hospitals and underwent a number of surgeries. The lessons I learned from these experiences have been put to good use time and again. Each new chance I have been granted has come with exciting opportunities. Once again, I had to venture out on my own to make my mark in the world, to once again try to fly.

After becoming disabled, I looked into the rehabilitation program offered by the state. Retraining for a 22–year–old ex–bartender/manager didn't appear on any lists, and nothing I was interested in did, either. A private company however, the Dale Carnegie Human Relations Program, offered a program in which I was interested.

This program was designed to give participants confidence and skills in public speaking and human relations. I just had to find the means to pay for it. The meager amount of Social Security Disability pay I received, $333.33 a month, barely kept me fed. I told the program counselor that while I thought the program was great and I would surely benefit from it, there was no way that I could afford to attend. I thanked him for his time and showed him to the door. Thinking that opportunity was gone, I went on with my day. The next day I received a call from the district manager of the program asking me if I would like to attend the classes. At first I was a little upset thinking this was a hard–pitch sell. *How dare they. I mean, man, I told them I was on SSDI. Were they really that hard up for attendees.* Holding back my anger I explained calmly to this gentleman that as much as I would like to participate, there was just no way I could on my limited income.

The next words he spoke were a wonderful surprise I will never forget. He said, "I didn't ask you if you could afford it. I asked would you like to attend?"

"Sure," I replied.

"Well then good. Be at the class tomorrow and don't worry about the cost. We have you covered. Will you be there?"

"Of course. Thank you." As I hung up the phone with a smile, I felt an energy flow through my being. It had been a long time since I had experienced mental challenges and I'd surely had enough of the physical ones for a while.

I was excited about being a part of this program and the entire event itself, for I'd had no opportunities to meet other people in a professional setting. Other than the occasional outings to the familiar local watering holes or gathering with family and friends, I rarely got out. I was ready to venture out on my own, expand my comfort zone, go new places, meet new people and learn new things. I realized I was starving for this and that it was important I succeed in this endeavor. I had to break free of my comfort zone.

Of course to get trapped in your comfort zone you don't have to be disabled. We all have to guard against getting complacent, or we may miss the chance to be part of great deeds and events that God has in store for us. It is my belief that God has many great and exciting opportunities for all of us to experience, but we must be able to show Him our love by always walking and stepping out in faith even when we are not certain of the path. If we do this He has assured us that as we walk through the doors of opportunity that He has opened we have nothing to fear and will succeed. "For the Lord watches over the way of the righteous, but the way of the wicked will perish" (Psalm 1:8). He promised through the blood of His Son, Jesus Christ, that he would walk with us. So I have and so I will.

The next evening I drove by myself to attend the first class at a major hotel in the great city of Chicago. As I drove, I avoided thinking of all the things that could go wrong with my being alone in a wheelchair. Although these thoughts were never too far in back in my mind, I knew if I prepared thoroughly, and I always did and still do, the fear of the unknown wouldn't stop me from reaching my goals. Every day is a risk just getting up, but we all do. Why? Because we are living out God's plan. And if we stay focused and prepare the best we can and never doubt that God is with us, we'll be okay.

After attending this program and meeting others who had far more fear in just trying to talk in front of a crowd than I ever did, I realized that we all have a disability of some form. Some disabilities just aren't visible. Sometimes the fear of being accepted or trying something new or having to change is more of a disability than one could imagine, but throughout our lives we all are confronted at some point in time with these fears. Some how, some way we must all overcome these fears or we become prisoners in our own minds. One young man, in the beginning of this class, trembled and sweated just standing in front of a crowd, let alone speaking. At the end of the course, he gave a heart–warming speech about his long–lost love. A woman who had stuttered for many years never stuttered once through her entire speech. Upon seeing these people succeed, I knew that I had been blessed. I no longer had the fear that would stop me from trying. The power and faith in me came from the belief in my God and I am thankful for the peace that I have been given and still have. Yet not all have that faith. Sadly, at that time, not even my own father had that faith. Fortunately, that would change.

After graduating on the evening of the last class many of the students decided to stay and celebrate. You know I wasn't going to pass up this good time, and all had a good time. Afterward I decided to visit an old friend who lived close by. It was a great reunion, but I had neglected to call home to let my family know. Since I had lived on my own prior to the accident and never had to report to anyone, it didn't even occur to me to report in. My independence was creeping back in as by all rights it should. But the next day I learned my father and mother had been frightened when I hadn't returned at the usual time and understandably so. In fact, my father had contacted friends on the police force and had an All Points Bulletin put out for me. The entire Chicago police force was looking for me. I thanked my parents for their concern and apologized for my thoughtlessness. I was so glad to have a father who cared for me and worried about me even though I too was an adult. Thinking about this incident still brings a smile to my face. This was one of the first times that they had to accept that I was nearing the time that I would once again have to leave the nest and fly on my own.

While I had a limited income, I often tried to make it grow in any way I could and sometimes, I must confess, in illegal ways. I had regrets about these shenanigans, but these regrets are far outweighed now by the blessings that God has given me. You have to know that there were many times I witnessed God's power and in those times gave my life to Him. Unfortunately, just the same there were many times that my worldly body took over and I fell into the trap of using alcohol and drugs.

The world is full of users. To see doctors, lawyers, and Indian chiefs partaking of legal and illegal mind–

altering substances was the norm. These were the days of liquid lunches and power ties. Many times because of this atmosphere I found myself lost, alone and searching for answers. All I had to do was turn back to God for the true answers to all my questions, my doubts, my fears, my dreams and my hope, but I didn't know this. Now I do know. My God is great because after thirty years of my turning back and forth, He once again opened His arms and is holding me close. Through His spirit He has taken away all my addictions, without my even having to try or think about it. That's right. Believe it or not, overnight the obsession to use was just lifted from me. I have listened and accepted without any doubt that He is Lord, and I continue to be obedient to His word. He is now blessing me with so much. That you are reading this book only confirms His glory.

Now please don't think that my days were all spent thinking how to make money illegally. Far from it. Most of the time I spent hours researching how to start a small business from my home. I succeeded in many businesses although they didn't always produce big earnings. Still, nothing ventured, nothing gained

One company I started was a T–shirt company I ran from my patio. That's right, with nothing but a phone and the gift of gab I started a company. After all, I had been a mechanic and a manager/bartender; how hard could being the president of a company be? It worked great. I would call big companies offering them T–shirts printed with their logo at a fair price. Now you ask how could this be? Well easy. Once I received the order over the phone, I would request their artwork. Then I would send this to a professional printer and negotiate a price that would assure me a small profit. Man, this T–shirt business was easy. It was going so well I even had thoughts of grandeur: to actually establish an office somewhere other than my patio. It really wasn't bad though. I had a table, phone, phonebook, sunshine, and I kept making sales. Have you ever heard the old saying, "Be careful what you ask for?" Well do so, because one day I asked for and received more than I wanted.

I made contact with a major company and convinced them that they needed to buy T–shirts from me. They did and did they ever! Ten thousand. Ten thousand. It was my largest order ever and after I filled it, the last order.

I forgot to take a few things into consideration. First, where was I going to get the up–front cash to purchase the T–shirts, and then where was I going to store them until printing time? Well it wasn't easy, but I made it happen and after having them printed and stored in every nook and cranny in the house waiting to be delivered I thought no problem. That was fun. What's next? I was looking forward to the day of delivery. Two days prior to the shipping date, I received a call from the buyer confirming that each T–shirt would be individually wrapped in its own plastic bag. Well, I had thrown these bags away, and no amount off discussion would change their minds. They wanted the bags.

Since the customer is always right, I had to bag the shirts. I commandeered all the friends and family I had, young and old, with the promise never to ask again or order any more shirts, period. We set forth to bag ten thousand stinking rotten good–for–nothing beautifully printed T–shirts. After some twenty–two hours of non–stop shifts along with a lot of muttering of how I should be drawn, quartered, tarred, and feathered, impaled upside down on a stick and left for the buzzards, the task was completed. Now, at this point if you don't think that the last thing I ever wanted to see, touch or smell in my life again was a T–shirt well, then you're sadly mistaken. The T–shirts were hand delivered to a grateful and pleased customer who never knew that the world had seen and heard the last of Transcendental Designs. But the world had not seen or heard the last of me. Far from it. This was only one of many ventures that I would pursue in the years to come, always learning more and more, always believing.

The time had come now that I wanted to move out on my own once again. But, in order to do this, I had to find a real job, one that paid a decent wage that would make it possible to live alone. It had been quite a few years since I had looked for and applied for a job, but I was excited because I had more confidence in myself than ever before, if you can believe that. The past was as if it had never happened. I now was known as a young man with a disability looking for a job.

With nothing but my looks and a certificate from Dale Carnegie I entered the office of a major binding company in a nearby city. In fact, it was the leader of the industry in those times. The company had invented much of the office binding equipment we use today. They were looking to fill a position of a telephone salesman. The job entailed contacting existing clients, furnishing them with supplies and giving equipment leads to the field salespersons. After having my second interview, in which I think the manager was more uncomfortable than I was, I was offered the job. Once again in those days rarely did people with disabilities just walk in or in my case, roll in, particularly to major corporations, and apply for jobs on their own. I'll never forget the remark the manager made when she hired me. She said, "I want you to know I didn't hire you because of your disability."

I replied, "Thank you but I didn't apply because I'm disabled."

With that she smiled and said, "I'll see you tomorrow." The ride home was exhilarating to say the least. I had found a job, and I couldn't wait to arrive home to share this great news. This job marked a new beginning. After a few paychecks I was ready to find my own place, which I did, not far from the job and a few miles from home. I rented the apartment and then it was time to move. As strange as it may seem, when I told my mother

I was moving out, she cried. And I knew why. She had to face her young man venturing out on his own again, a young man who would have to face even more difficult challenges than the first time he left home.

"Mom, don't cry," I said. "You know the time has come. Your love and care have made this time possible. You know there is nothing I can't do. I just don't walk very well." With this she smiled and hugged me. She knew just as I did that it was because of God's will it was my time to try, time to fly.

> For the Mighty One has done great things for me;
> and holy is His name.
>
> Luke 1:49 (KJV)

JUST DO IT

Of all the lessons I've learned living on my own, the most important was to be prepared for the unexpected and able to adapt and overcome. Just like anyone else I had to complete all the necessary chores of keeping and maintaining a clean home. I faced many obstacles in doing this, but with some little adaptations I could overcome them.

One of the most time–consuming and challenging tasks was grocery shopping. Pushing the cart while rolling wasn't too bad although my strength and endurance were tested after the cart was full. Now as I've come to the autumn of my years, such chores are more challenging. I thank God for giving me a woman who loves and cares about me and shares in the pushing of the cart. I love her so. Okay, back to the story.

I always requested of the grocery baggers that they not fill bags too full and that they tie a knot in each bag so that when I carried the bags inside, my teeth wouldn't fall out. What! Your teeth you say! Think about it. How do you roll and carry a bag? You don't. So I carried my groceries just like a cat carries her kittens. It works. Carrying groceries up the steep ramp leading to the door of my new apartment was tricky too, especially in a snowstorm. The thought of hauling each bag up one at a time just didn't cut it. It would have taken many trips and it was too cold and wet to be playing outside. What would I do? What would I do? Adapt and overcome! I found an old box, tied a rope around it, filled it with groceries and dragged it up the ramp from the warm, dry entry way. An instant escalator. I have dreamed up many creative solutions to problems through the years. And even though I have strived for total independence, I am never ashamed or too proud to ask for help when the need arises. This too was a lesson that I had to learn. It wasn't the easiest, but I discovered we must never believe that we are self—made men and women. Such a belief is terribly selfish. All through our lives we are blessed with someone who is willing to share the load and lend a hand. Fathers, mothers, sisters, brothers, friends, and God help us every day. Right? So how can we ever say we did anything by ourselves. So don't be afraid to lend a hand, not even to a person with a disability. I mention this because so many people are wary of asking a person with a disability if they can assist. Don't be. Even though I can do many things on my own, I appreciate the fact that someone cares enough to ask. If I don't need any assistance at the time, I will kindly thank you for asking and this gives me the opportunity to share with you how I do certain tasks on my own, like putting Pegasus in the car, or hauling groceries, or changing a flat tire, or riding a motorcycle, or jumping out of an airplane, or swimming. The last three I'll explain a little later. No matter what, don't forget one of God's commandments is to love thy neighbor. I feel truly blessed to have had so many who have cared enough to lend a hand and so many opportunities to share my love and my experience about being disabled with others. I even had the opportunity to go back and visit patients at Marionjoy. How strange this was. I felt so much power and faith when I returned that I wanted to share this with those who were facing the same difficult challenges that I already had faced and overcome.

As I looked around upon entering the therapy room in which I had spent so many grueling hours fighting for and achieving my independence, I saw faces expressing pain, sorrow, determination, and hope. Even more than before, my belief in a higher power, my God, was alive and working. The more times I visited and sat with young boys and girls and old men and women, helping them to see that it was possible to live their lives with their disabilities and to encourage them to fight through the pain, the stronger I became.

One day I received a call from one of the staff nurses who was a dear friend asking if I could come and visit a seventeen-year-old boy who had suffered the same type of accident and paralysis as I did. She told me he was not willing to attempt rehab, and if he continued to refuse, they would have to discharge him and send him home—or to a nursing facility. They just couldn't let a bed be wasted, especially when there were so many others who wanted and needed the chance to receive therapy. The boy had told the nurse that in one year he was going to walk out of the center on his own, so he needn't work out.

When I went to visit this young man, I saw myself lying there. The expression on his face was the same one that my parents and family must have seen on my face so many years before. I could see the strength he was using to fight back the fear, a strength he didn't even know he had. As I approached his bedside without any acknowledgment on his part whatsoever, I said a silent prayer asking God to give me the words that would help me help this young man. I introduced myself and tried to strike up some sort of conversation. Although he was polite, he never turned to look at me. At that moment I felt a powerful urge to turn and leave. I mean, what was I doing here? I was no counselor or therapist. Why should I think I was qualified to help this man? What should I say? Then the words came. "You know, my little buddy, I know what you're going through," I said. This was not just a line, and I told him so. "Many people—doctors, family, friends, will say this, but they really don't know. How could they? But you see I can because I too have had the same kind of accident you had, and I too have had to endure the same kind of injuries. I know that the rehab you receive here is of great help and will make you stronger and able to be independent with your disability and if you don't try they will kick you out of this joint."

At this point, he finally turned his eyes toward me and said. "Thanks so much for coming to visit and taking the time to talk with me and you are probably right about how great a place this is, but you see I don't need therapy because in a year I am going to be able to walk out of here on my own. So why work out now?"

Well, let me tell you, this threw me a bit. How do you respond to such conviction? Who am I to say this isn't so? Have I not said many times how great God is? Do I myself not believe that all things are possible if you believe in Him? To this I responded, "That's great, but in the meantime you should prepare for that day." "There is no need. Didn't you hear what I said? In one year I will walk again. So why don't you just leave me alone?" he replied.

Well, my dear readers, what I said next came as a shock even to me. You see I do believe that God can do great things, and that Jesus did heal many with just his belief. I believe that God does hear your prayers, but He does not always answer them the way we want Him to and we should not question why. I also believe that what I have experienced because of my disability is for a reason and to be here for this young man was one of the reasons.

"Hey! I'll leave, but I'm not going until you tell me why you get to walk in one year and I don't? You had the same accident as me, you are paralyzed just like me, and there is no medical procedure that will make either one of us walk ever again. So if you want to waste your time and the time of those who are willing to help you then you go right ahead. But let me tell you, I don't want to be the bearer of bad news, but you have to hear this and know this. I am sorry, but you and I are not going to walk again. So you better start working on getting stronger or you're just going to wither away and die. Is that what you want?" I said. With this he turned towards me with tears streaming down his face and my heart sank.

Oh my, what have I done? What right did I have to say such words to this boy? Nobody invited me here. Can I be sued for acting like a counselor with no degree? Oh, my dear little buddy, forgive me for hurting you. I never meant this to be. I only wanted to help you. Please forgive me if I hurt you. What he said next I'll never forget and once again, I know God is all around and guiding us.

He grabbed my hand and sobbing he said, "No! You didn't hurt me, you have helped me and you did what no one else had the guts to do. That was to tell me the truth and I thank you."

At that moment as I hugged him close, I felt the power of God flowing through both of us. I knew he would be all right and I told him so. A few days later I received another call from my nurse friend. With great excitement in her voice, she thanked me and said, "I don't know what you said or did, but whatever it was, it worked. Ever since you met with him he has been working out more than we could have hoped for and is doing great. Can I ask what you told him?" With joy in my heart I said, "I told him to believe in God for He is true, and to just do it!"

> For truly my words are not false; One who is perfect in knowledge is with you.
>
> Job 36:4 (KJV)

ONE LUMP OR TWO

Chin to chest, just remember chin to chest. Yeah! Easy to say, not always easy to do. And why would you want to? Well, if you were a prizefighter you would keep your chin tucked so as to be able to absorb a punch to your head. If you were a gymnast you would tuck it in order to do a successful somersault. If you are in a wheelchair you better learn and learn fast to tuck your chin to your chest when you have the unfortunate and by no means occasional thrill of tipping backwards in your wheelchair. If you tuck your head correctly, you will avoid the gut wrenching, teeth–rattling, eye–popping, ear–ringing, stargazing, bird chirping that follows bouncing your head off the ground. Unlike those who train for a championship fight or practice their tumbling techniques, I had to perfect this art without ever wanting to try. It is just so hard to make yourself fall backwards in order to practice. Nevertheless, I was able to graduate with high honors and many awards and a member in high standing with the fraternity Ya Banga Yourhead Alotta, from the School of Hard Knocks. Many years ago, way before I knew of wheelchairs and

Stryker beds, way before there was a politically correct way to speak of people with disabilities, there was a man who came to visit us at our school. This man used a wheelchair for mobility and played on a wheelchair basketball team. It seemed in those years this was the only sport that the disabled attempted. It led to the profiling of people in wheelchairs. If you used a wheelchair, surely, you must play basketball. This man explained the importance of the handles on the wheelchair, the handles on the back that are used to push a person. What I learned (not really caring at the time unaware of how important this lesson would be for me later) was that these handles also served as shock absorbers of sorts. When you fell backwards, if you tucked your chin to your chest, the handles would hit first, hopefully, before the back of your head.

As he demonstrated this, I thought, "Yeah, that does seem to work, glad I don't have to deal with it." Of course, at the time I did not know what my future held or how right he was.

Now, as a graduate from the School of Hard Knocks, I have become an expert of sorts on bumps and lumps. If you ran your fingers over my head you would feel this to be so. Without a doubt, concrete is not as hard as ice. And as for grass being soft, well, just think of the vine that covers the brick wall in the outfield of Wrigley Field. It appears to be soft and green and luscious, but when you hit it, you still hit bricks.

Those who join the fraternity are always determined to learn to pop a wheelie. It's like a sign of initiation. Like so many others, I practiced finding that small sweet spot, the point where you are on two wheels free falling and by merely breathing, you could rock ever so slightly like a fine–tuned pendulum. Once I accomplished this daring feat, I was called to try more death defying tricks, like some crazed daredevil, never fearing or thinking of the consequences. There was the How–Long–Can–You–Balance trick, the How–Far–Can–You–Go–On–Two–Wheels trick, or my favorite, the Turn–On–Two trick. Then, when you mastered these, it was time to take it up a notch. Let's try popping a wheelie while going down a curb. Now, if you were able to successfully accomplish this feat, not only were you recognized as a wheelie–popper extraordinaire, but you also had a practical skill. In days past, curb cuts and ramps did not exist. So the wheelie popped while going down a curb enabled you to travel and cross streets that were otherwise impassable. After perfecting this feat, nothing could stop you, not even stairs.

Stairs? Are you crazy? What do you mean stairs? This is the one thing for certain that people in wheelchairs can't climb, but it doesn't mean you can't go down them if you really want to. I have hit my head going down steps so often it's a wonder I can still speak clearly. And those spots in my eyes, well, they don't seem to be as big anymore. I hope I never have to have chemotherapy because I'm certain my bald head would look like the surface of Mars.

It seemed that the times I did take a hit, there was always an innocent bystander close by, amazed at what they saw or thought they saw. One time I was exiting my friend's patio door, which entailed the wheelie pop with a forward thrust, not a very difficult move (maybe a four on the scale). However, I didn't allow for the added ridge from the sliding door runners, which increased the difficulty to a six. As I came out the door, it happened. From the ground, I looked up. My hands rubbed the back of my head, and my ears rang from the resounding thump of my head connecting with the concrete patio deck. As my eyes focused and the blue of the sky came into view, I saw a small face staring down at me and heard a tiny voice.

"Hey, mister, can I see the snake?" Still rubbing my skull and not really comprehending what was being said, I heard once again, "Hey, mister, can I see the snake?" Now reality struck.

I really didn't need any extra excitement at this point you know. I was on my back looking up, and I asked, what snake? I started looking back and forth for the snake. Not seeing one, but unsure that there might be one nearby, I asked again with a grimace, what snake?

At that moment I was to know the innocence of a child. Whereas most adults would have looked at me wondering how they may help or if I hurt, what is this child seeing? In the room was a glass terrarium filled with plants and rocks and in the imagination of this boy a huge snake. So the opened door provided easy access, other than having to climb over my body, to finally see the snake that surely must be in that terrarium. Relieved that a snake was not close to my head, I made it known there was no snake, there had never been a snake, nor would there ever be a snake in that terrarium. With that he turned in disgust and left. Oh, how blue the sky looks.

Another fine time was when my friend and I were driving through the park and down a steep hill toward the river. Now I must admit I really don't know what possessed me to do what I was going to do next.

"Stop the car! Stop the car," I yelled. As we stopped at the top of this giant hill, I turned towards my friend and said, "meet me at the bottom. I'm going to roll down from here."

Being the close friend that he was, he looked at me and said, *sure.*

There I sat atop my gallant steed. My hands released my grip and the wind rushed through my hair as I sped down the paved hill towards the river. Ahhh, the rush, the freedom, the speed.

I can do it. Look at me, I'm flying… I'm flying like an eagle! Yeah! I neared the end of the run, only a few feet from the bottom. I did it. I'm the coolest. Surely no one has ever gone this far or this fast. Man, I'm flying so fast the wheels are shaking like crazy! The wheels are shaking like crazy.

As I saw the wheel fly off, I remember seeing the asphalt parallel to my body. *Hey! I really am flying. Isn't that Pegasus going by?* As I came to a crumpled stop only a few feet from the end of the run, I heard once again the sweet voice of a concerned child.

"Hey mister, are you going to do that again? Cause if you are I want to go get my brother."

As my friend lifted Pegasus and me into the car, I waved to the crowd. Sorry folks, show's over, the monkey is dead. As crazy as you may think all this to be, these lumps and bumps were necessary in the big scheme of things. They created a sense of self-confidence that opened the doors to many adventures. One of these was being able to once again ride a motorcycle. That's right! When I traveled to the National Wheelchair games in Seattle, I met a man who had designed a specially built motorcycle for persons who used wheelchairs. When I saw the bike, I asked if I could ride it and when? The opportunity was given the following day. After meeting with the designer of this unique invention, I asked why he had not marketed this bike sooner. He explained that it had been stored away for over five years. He had originally designed it for his close friend who had suffered a spinal cord injury. After going through the painstaking work of creating the machine, he found his friend did not appreciate the bike because of his poor attitude and anger towards the world for having to face the rest of his life disabled. The designer grew angry and thought that all people who were disabled were jerks and probably had the same poor attitudes. Thankfully for me, and many others, he met another person with the same disability who was positive and stressed the fact that not all persons with disabilities thought like his friend. He said it would be a shame if the inventor did not offer this item to those who believed, had faith and the power and confidence to keep on trying, no matter the situation.

Glory goes to God for sending another person to show this man a new way to look at people with disabilities, because now at the age of 26, I own such a bike. Picture if you will a motorcycle and next to it a chariot. He used an automatic bike and attached this rig next to it and then moved the handlebars off the bike and attached them to the cart. To get on the chariot I would pop a small wheelie up and then strap Pegasus and myself in. The passenger would sit on the motorcycle with a small handle to hang on to as I sped away. It was quite a sight, and since I was one of the only person that had one in the Midwest, I was approached by what seemed like every newspaper and news show in the Chicago–land area. Even though this bike was street legal, many police officers and troopers stopped me just because they couldn't believe their eyes. Riding it was quite a thrill and gave me more reason to try other adventures. One beautiful summer morning I was taking a ride through the countryside. I did not have a care in the world. Mile after mile the bike hummed as I did. The wind was warm, and the sky was a beautiful blue with dots of red and white and … what the heck is that? As I watched the colors draw closer, I could make out parachutes. Four or five chutes newly opened drifted towards the ground and me. As I turned to follow them, I could see the small airport and the drop–zone where they were headed. Turning off the bike I waited and as I watched them glide to and fro, I thought how cool it must be to jump from a plane, something I had always wanted to do. As the jumpers landed and strolled toward the hanger, I drove close and asked, "Hey, is there a jump master around that could answer a question?"

"Sure is," one jumper replied. "He's coming in for a landing right now." Here we go again. Not knowing what possessed me, I rode toward him.

As he came closer, I asked, "Can I jump?" The look on his face was one of disbelief, and then it changed to intrigue. We introduced ourselves.

"I have never jumped with a person that used a wheel-chair or any man that has the guts to ride a motorcycle in a chair. I'm one of the national champion skydivers, and if I can't make it happen, no one can. So let's talk," he said.

The preparation to attempt a fifteen thousand feet freefall was really not as extensive as one may think. All I had to remember was to pull the cord and be limber when I hit. Well, I had the limber part down pat. We had discussed options on how I was going to land. The first thought is I would attempt to land in water. Although a nice soft spot I really didn't think I wanted to be in water with heavy boots and a chute with many strings wrapped around me. You may think I'm crazy, but I'm not stupid. The next suggestion was that we would have a group of men catch me on a ten feet by ten feet mat. Yeah that's the ticket, a mat. They explained that they would strap a walkie–talkie to my arm and guide me down, right to the mat. Although I had never jumped before, I had all the confidence in the world in both of the instructors, so I decided why not. Sounds easy enough. What could go wrong? Now, I know many of you readers, especially you moms, are saying, "Well, you could break your neck." Yeah, but I already did.

"Rich! It's a million–to–one chance you die the first time you jump," said a good friend of mine who was an ex–Ranger. "And if you do, you're just an unlucky person and you would probably get hit by a bus the next day, so might as well jump." I prepared to jump the following week. Many of my friends and family, although uneasy about my jump, came out to watch. It was a picnic atmosphere, but because of the weather, the jump was postponed. The jump master insisted on perfectly clear, calm skies, so with that everyone packed up for the long ride home. I imagine many were relieved thinking I would have a change of heart before the next weekend came. Not true.

Early the following Saturday, we would again caravan to the drop sight and I prepared to jump. However, because of other commitments the crowd was quite a bit smaller. Now there were only a couple of friends, my sister, and my stouthearted mother. God bless her. I knew she was frightened for me, but she never showed it. She just told me I was crazy, but because of the strength that I gained from her, she knew her baby boy at the age of twenty–four was going to go through with it no matter what, so she never once told me not to. Its been three years since mom went home. I love and miss her very much.

Now wouldn't you know after spending hours at the airport, we once again were told, no jump. Drat! Back we go. Many would take this as a sign that maybe I shouldn't attempt this feat, but by now you should know that nothing was going to stop me from jumping. So with a nod and a wave, I said I would see them next week and I did. The following Saturday I was heading out, but to my dismay no one was able to join me. This couldn't be. There has to be someone to see this and record what happens. With a little explanation, a small guilt trip and a promise he could have my new car if anything happened to me, I convinced my best friend to accompany me even though it was against his better judgment. Today was going to be the day. The weather was perfect for a jump, clear skies, no wind to speak of, and a mild temperature. I donned my jumpsuit, goggles, helmet, and most importantly my parachute, shook my friend's hand and prepared to board the plane. Much to my surprise he grabbed me and gave me a big hug.

"Hey," I said, "don't worry. I'll be back in a few minutes. Don't go anywhere with my car." It was about a half hour flight up to fifteen thousand feet. The two instructors, positioned in the back of the four–seat plane, went over the exit plan with me. I was seated with my back to the dashboard to the right of the pilot and my left shoulder touched the exit door. The pilot winked at me with a smile as the door flew upwards and open. *Oh my, this is it. My goodness, I can see clouds and the houses look, well, like ants.* I sat inches from the open door and wide–open spaces. *Man, Rich, don't fall out yet.* I grabbed the seat belt of the pilot to make sure this would not happen.

The first perilous part of this stunt was to exit the plane and kneel on a two–foot strut under the wing. The first instructor climbed past me and out, hanging onto the wing support with one foot on the furthest edge of the strut. Next, I was positioned with my feet dangling out of the craft and held by a secure grip of the other instructor. The trick was to grab the support, swing toward the strut, and take a kneeling position. This went smoother than you may think. You see, my legs were taped together with Duct tape in order to keep them from splitting apart upon impact. This along with the wind acted as a small rudder and enabled me to position easily. What a thrill. Can you believe this? Looking inside the plane, I saw the pilot grinning ear to ear with disbelief at the sight of me hanging and flying outside of a plane fifteen thousand feet over the countryside. Let me tell you, there is no greater thrill. The only thing close is riding a super roller coaster backwards. As I waited for the signal to let go and fly, I looked around. *God, how beautiful the world is.* With a nod of a head and a quick silent prayer I leaned back and tumbled into the sky. *Arch your back, arch your back.* That was the first command I learned and followed. By doing this, the law of physics took over and the uncontrolled tumbling became a controlled freefall. It was a strange sensation. Falling well over a hundred miles per hour, I felt like I had dropped off the edge of a roller coaster. Other than my cheeks flapping and my ears bombarded by the sound of the wind rushing by, I just felt like I was floating on a big beautiful cloud. We fell five thousand feet. Even though it felt like a long time, I'm sure it was only a few minutes. When the time came to open the chute, the instructors who had flown with me all this time now took hold of the cord and gave a tug. Faster then a blink of an eye the chute shot out towards the heavens pulling me with incredible speed hundreds of feet back up. Or so it felt. In reality, what happened was that I stopped fast. The next command I learned and followed was to look up. This was most important because I needed and wanted to make sure the chute was opened fully. Since I'm here to type this, you know it did. After realizing that I was safe up to this point, I reached up and placed my hands in the little stirrups that controlled the movement of the parachute. Through my screams of utter joy I heard a voice come over the walkie–talkie.

"Hey Rich! How are you doing?"

"Everything looks fine from here."

"What I would like you to do now is to learn how to control the parachute. I'm going to ask you to do a few things. First I would like you to pull down on the right cord." As I did this I swung in a half circle to the right. The feeling was indescribable. Here I was thousands of feet above the earth with my legs dangling in the wind. At one point I was asked to pull both cords at the same time and hold. This stopped me in mid space. There was no movement and total silence. The feeling was so unique, all I could do was yell with joy. As I continued my descent, I marveled at the sight never thinking about what was to come next. Then it hit me. *Hey it's almost time to land. I wonder how this is going to be.* As I gazed toward the ground that now seemed to be approaching faster than it was a moment ago, I could see the group of men that surrounded the ten feet by ten feet mat. As I watched from above, I thought of how the Keystone coppers looked when they ran all amok. And at that moment I knew there was no way they were ever going to catch me. Now up to this point I never really felt as if I was falling and had no awareness of the speed either. There was nothing to relate to in space. Once I saw the treetops, I knew I was in for a rude awakening. By the time I realized I was at the top of the highest tree in the land I had hit the ground only a few feet from the mat that they had thrown towards me in hopes of somehow breaking and comforting my fall.

I had hit my head many times in my life, but this could only compare to being thrown off a roof head first and hard. My friend Saul told me later he thought I was surely dead or going to be.

"Man! Your head slapped the ground like I never saw before and then bounced. I'm surprised there wasn't a dent in the ground." Who knows, there may have well been. All I could hear through my plugged up ears was, "Hey Rich, how are you?"

Because I'd had the wind knocked out of me, all I could utter was a weak, but positive *whooo*. That was enough to let them know and myself that I made it.

Now I would be recognized as one of the only quadriplegics in this country and perhaps the world that successfully did a free fall and hit the ground. Haven't heard of any since, and by the grace of God, I still look forward to doing it again. Why not? There's nothing I can't do right? To be quite honest, I have never regretted all these lumps and bumps I have taken because they meant gaining independence. This independence I gained was not without a cost, but because of the faith and strength that God gave me, I was willing to pay it. How much did you say? One lump or two!

> Many, O Lord my God, are the wonders, which
> You have done.
>
> Psalm 40:5(KJV)

SINK OR SWIM

The opportunities that I received to help others were real blessings. The many times I visited patients was truly a gift from God. Even though many times I left the premises with a lump in my throat and a tear in my eye, there was always renewed faith and joy in my heart. This joy came from helping others in a time of need. It has been said and I have found it to be true that when you are facing challenges and feel that there is no hope and nothing good is happening for you, the best cure and the greatest way to change this attitude is to help someone else with their problems. What? I have to be a nut you say. No, it's true. It works. I have seen its miraculous effect on others, and me, but also I know this to be true because this is what Jesus taught us.

"That so you give of yourself you to shall be given." All God asked of all of us is to love thy neighbor and to know that there are many others who are worse off than me and you and have no hope or belief and even sadder no one to care about them to share the Word of God. Because of my efforts as I previously stated, I was given many blessings. One of these was the chance to do something that I had loved to do and thought I would never do again and had not done for over five years and that was to swim.

One afternoon while visiting at the center a lady approached me who worked there, and asked if I ever swam before the accident. I replied that I had and even scuba–dived occasionally, but that I had not since the accident.

"Would you like to learn to swim again?" she asked.

"Swim again? Me swim again how? Can I?"

"Sure you can and if you meet me here on Saturday, I'll show you. Okay?"

"Yeah, sure I'll be there." As I drove home, I could hardly believe what I'd heard. Swim again. I'm going to learn to swim again. Prior to the accident I was an avid swimmer and scuba diver, but since then I hadn't ventured into a pool unless I was wearing a life vest, rubber duck, or some other sort of flotation device and I never went alone. The thought of once again being able to enjoy the summer with all its water activities thrilled me. To be able to swim in a lake or go to the beach and feel the power of the ocean's surf tossing me to and fro was incomprehensible. How could it be possible? Although no one ever told me this, I imagined that if I entered the water, I would sink like a rock. The weight of my dead legs that I had to pull around led me to believe this. You have to understand in these days there were not many disabled individuals that I'd heard of doing sports other than basketball, so where would I learn differently. Accessible housing or transportation let alone the Americans with Disabilities Act were far away dreams yet to be realities. Nevertheless, that Saturday morning within five minutes of entering the pool I knew I would no longer have to fear drowning in a pool again.

I, along with three other brothers–in–arms, frolicked and splashed in the water like newborn ducks watchful of the mother duck, our soon–to–be coach. It still amazes me to this day how buoyant my body is. I can even float with my arms crossed, and if I desire, sleep on the water without sinking. This fact along with a few minor alterations of head placement in the water enabled us to learn to freestyle stroke through the water without the use of our legs. So every chance we had to make use of the pool we did. Now when I say pool, I must make it clear that this pool was no more then a glorified tub. It was no more than twelve feet long, six feet wide and four feet deep. You see this pool had never been used for any other reason than to give patients a chance to feel the warmth and have a break from the pressure of sitting in a wheelchair or to assist the seniors in strengthening their legs until we began swimming in it. Each of us worked hard at perfecting our strokes. We then found ourselves racing each other for fun across the pool, and without our knowledge, the therapist was timing us. Although I'm sure it must have looked comical to others watching three guys swim back and forth in this tub like we were Olympic swimmers, in our own minds we were Olympians.

After many weeks the therapist told us that we were swimming at the pace of those who were competing in the National Wheelchair Games.

"Hey, why don't you guys try out for the qualifying state finals that are coming up in a few months?" Well, the tide in the pool had definitely turned. Without any hesitation, and an agreement that she would be our coach, we agreed to train for competition and I did.

Actually trying out for state competition was a goal I thought that I never would attempt, let alone qualifying for competition. I told myself not to get carried away with the dream of going into the National Wheelchair Games. But man, the thought sure did enter my mind and I dreamt of winning a medal the first year. Impossible! Or was it?

Now in order to be able to compete in the state games I had to secure a spot in time tryouts. I had to be able to swim a twenty-five meter race in under fifty seconds, but to win a medal in nationals I would have to do this in under thirty five seconds and with only one breath of air. That's right, one breath of air. You may ask why only one breath of air? Well, I'll tell you why. Because the gold medal winner for the last two years did it on, Yep! that's right, one breath of air. This game was no longer child's play, but serious competition. That meant serious training not just frolicking in a pool. So now the question came, how bad did I want it? By the blood of my father and mother I am a Mexican not a Mexi–can't. I decided I wanted it bad! So bad, that for the next six months I prepared and set a training routine that was as strict as one could imagine. Champions are not born; they are made. So it began.

I started my mornings at six o'clock a.m. with a blended chocolate milk drink with four raw eggs and a handful of vitamins. After donning my sweatsuit and strapping my gloves to my hands with tape and adorning Pegasus and myself with tin foil reflectors so all the able bodies (AB's) that were driving could see me. I started out with quick five or six–mile jaunts. Usually I would return by ten o'clock or so depending on the direction of the wind. After resting for an hour or so and having a high–protein lunch, I would make for my weight room, which was wall papered with posters of Superman, Hulk, Aztec warriors, and the like. Plenty of mirrors hung on the wall too, so that I could look myself in the eyes and yell, "no pain, no gain" and I did it. For two or three hours I would lift weights, always with a goal in sight, a medal. Now if you think that was it for the day, you're sadly mistaken because how could you train for swimming competition if you didn't swim, right? So after a couple of hours rest, including a nap, I would once again don my workout clothes with high tech reflectors and head for the high school pool. Situated about a mile away from home, I started my swimming regimen that lasted two hours or so, depending on how much water I swallowed gasping for air, or how many times I bellied up as I crossed the twenty–five–meter pool. Each night I arrived home somewhere between eight and eight–thirty, showered, then headed to bed for a good night's rest. At dawn I started all over again. After many weeks of this training I sometimes would think if I was nuts.

"What makes me think I am going to qualify, let alone win," I asked myself. The current athletes who were competing had been training for years. I was able to clear the pool under fifty seconds, but not by much and only on good days which were few and far between. I wasn't even close to clearing the pool in under thirty–five seconds let alone on one breath of air without passing out. So who was I kidding? But each night as I watched those black markers on the bottom of the pool go by and I listened to my air bubbles, I would say: "You can do it, you can do it, by the power that God has given you. You will do it!" I believed and I never stopped believing. Even when others didn't and let me tell you this does happen.

Watch out for those people who try to convince you that your dream is impossible. Steer clear of them. Be aware there are many out there, and sometimes they are your closest friends. If you do happen to come across them, let them know that all things are possible when you believe in God and His glory. It happened to me. I would like to share with you a discussion that took place with a dear friend of mine who, for whatever reason, just couldn't find it in his heart to believe in the power of God and his Word. As we grew up together from boyhood to manhood, we shared many crazy times. We lived, laughed, loved, lied, cried, and sometimes nearly died together. I am proud to have been his friend and to know now that he has grown to be a great man, a loving caring father and husband and has come to know of Christ.

But this was not always the case. In our younger wilder days he was a man of his own means. He answered to no one, let alone God. No, far from it. He thought that man made his own way and he could handle any situation by his own strength. I must confess in those days I had some of those same thoughts, but after facing what I have since then and after have experienced the blessings of God, that way was no longer my way of thinking. Without a doubt I knew better. Even though my friend had been with me since the time of the accident and had seen so many times how I had been blessed since, he still refused to accept that it was not my strength alone that made me who I was but God's. One day as we talked, he asked me why he should believe as I do. Being such a close friend, he was angry for me that God did these things to me. He wanted to know how I could believe that my strength alone is not what kept me alive and continuing to strive. He wanted to know why I felt there was a higher power that kept me alive and continuing to strive—and not just my own will. To this question, a question that has been asked by many others since then, my reply was guided by the Word of

God. My dear brother, what if one day you and I were on a ship in the ocean many miles from shore and it sank. As we swam for our lives to shore, we grew tired. We swam many miles and even though we had only one more mile to go, we could swim no more. We had no strength left. We were floundering in the water and knew that we were going to drown and sink. With the shore and safety in our sights, I would lift my voice to God and use my last ounce of strength and last breath to ask God for the strength to swim one more mile. What would you do? Sink or swim?

> Greater is He that is in you, than He that is in the world.
>
> I John 4:4 (KJV)

INCH BY INCH,
ONE FOOT AT A TIME

Nine hundred and sixty inches. That's all. A mere nine hundred and sixty inches. It seems like such a short distance. But imagine if you were an inchworm clearing one inch per second without a rest. It would take you sixteen minutes and you would have traveled eighty–five feet. I felt like an inchworm as I trained for competition. My goal was to travel twenty–five meters through water on one breath of air, doing the most grueling stroke in competitive swimming, the butterfly, and without the use of my legs. And I had to do it under thirty–five seconds. Believe it or not this was how it had to be in order to win a medal in the nationals. Each night as I fell to sleep exhausted from the day's training, I dreamt of how it would be to compete and win. The thought of being in front of a cheering crowd listening to the loudspeaker calling me to come forward and accept my medal was a dream that I soon would try to make reality.

It was the spring of a new year. April showers brought May flowers and the Central State Wheelchair Games.

This was it, the first chance to prove ourselves against hundreds of other athletes all competing for the ultimate prize, securing a place in the nationals in June. My comrades and I worked hard at bettering our times and perfecting our strokes. I spent countless hours in the pool doing lap after lap, never seeing more than the black markers on the bottom of the pool, counting each one awaiting the hardness of the tiled wall hearing only the beat of my heart pounding against my ever-straining lungs that longed for one more breath. Occasionally I heard through the bubbles passing me the chant of onlookers giving me the spirit and desire to keep going. But training time was coming to an end; May was here. We had rallied, along with many others in the community, to raise funds to send the four of us to the state finals and represent Marionjoy. But wait, how could we? We didn't even have a name or colors to wear.

"Hey, how about the "Marionjoy Manta Rays," I suggested. And with a unanimous vote and a shout, "yeah, that's cool," we became the Manta Rays. All we needed now were colors. After a few calls to my friends in the printing business I was able to secure warm-up suits for all. They were beautiful light blue jackets with matching pants. On the sides were thin blue and red stripes from heel to waist and cuff to neck. Imprinted on the back, in their entire splendor, were the words Marianjoy Manta Rays. What a sight! As I presented them to the team the day before we left for competition, there was a shout of glee with a batch of *oohs* and *ahhs* thrown in. But then, as we all donned our suits, I heard a sound of horror.

"Oh no! Oh no!"

"What?" I screamed. "What do you mean *oh no*. What?" Through all the excitement, no one had noticed until now that the name Marionjoy was misspelled Marianjoy on the jackets. Oh man, an A instead of an O. Let me tell you, at that moment, I felt this was a disaster. I felt as if someone had stuck their hand in my chest and ripped my heart out. We all felt the shock and horror.

"Okay don't anybody worry. Leave it to me. I'll have this fixed in no time," I assured them. You know there will always be trials and tribulations in life. Some are smaller than others, but no matter what, they will come. What's important is how you handle these trials that test your faith and show your belief to others. The first rule is believe and don't panic; believe and it can be done.

Throughout my business career I have found that success depends not on how much you know or how well you may plan, but how you react in the few moments when all has failed and the clock is ticking. With less than fourteen hours left before the state finals, somehow, someway, the silk–screened jackets had to be changed. I made numerous phone calls and found that there would be no way to purchase new jackets in time or reprint the ones we had, but something had to be done. What could we do? Like the old saying goes, back to the drawing board.

I gathered up the suits and headed for the print shop to brainstorm in hopes of devising a way to change an A to an O. After a bit of roaming around the shop searching for an idea, it hit. We found some old iron–on patches that we embroidered and cut and covered the silk screened letters leaving us with a still splendid looking jacket and hours to spare. The next morning the Manta Rays, donned in colors and looking every bit as athletes, set off amidst the cheering of family, friends, and staff, to compete in our first Wheelchair Games. This was a most exciting day not only because of the event, but also because we would be seeing and interacting with hundreds of others who had disabilities. And let me tell you, even to me this was quite an eye opening experience.

Upon arriving at the university where the games were held, we were directed to the registration hall where we would be tested by a group of physicians to determine and certify our level of disabilities. It was quite a sight. The room buzzed with excitement as hundreds of athletes with all types of disabilities awaited their turns. Some were using wheelchairs, some crutches, some had one leg, some had no legs, and some had even less. But one thing we all had in common was that we were disabled, but able. We were all athletes. We had all trained hard. We all wanted to race and we all wanted to win, but we all cared about each other, too. When I think back to why this was so, I believe it was because we all had to face the fact that we were disabled in a world that did not recognize persons with disabilities as being able. Yeah, that's right. We were second–class citizens. We were looked upon as a burden to society. Society didn't really care about us. How sad a place the world was then. One of the first commandments we are asked to follow is to love your neighbor as you would yourself. Sadly, few people follow this commandment.

If my accident had occurred five years earlier than it did, I would have been placed in a nursing center for long term care without any rehab services at all. If I had lived in the Old West and broken my neck falling from my horse, I most likely would have been given one last cigarette and a shiny bullet. But now I was among hundreds of people who were out to show the country we were winners in all ways.

As I looked around the room, I finally realized that I was not alone in this disabled life. All fears that I had experienced and challenges I had overcome were shared by many. Each of us knew the power and strength we all had that we were all blessed in some way. We were even able to laugh about what we had gone through and who we were.

I'll never forget the first time I was categorized as a person with a disability, and not in the politically correct way as we have been taught in present times. We all were taking a break from the day and gathered in the recreation area. Some were sitting around talking, others watching TV, and some shooting pool. This was one game I was very good at, but had not tried sitting in a wheelchair. I watched others shooting from this position. Then the doors swung open and I turned to see a man built like a brick house, a perfect V–shaped torso as wide as the door, standing there. Though his upper body was perfect, he walked with crutches. Now when I say he walked with crutches, I don't mean like you would if you had a broken leg. No! He literally walked with crutches because his legs were not fully formed. They swung only a foot from his waist and could never support him, so he walked with crutches. When I saw this, I couldn't believe the strength, both physically and mentally, he displayed. Upon entering, he looked over at the guys shooting pool in wheelchairs.

"Hey, get off the table. Gimps can't shoot pool."

Oh my, what did he just say? Gimps? Gimps! As laughter broke the silence, I thought, it's true. I am now a gimp. Can you beat that. Of all the things I had been called in my life, I would have never thought that someday I would be known as a gimp. Now I think how proud I am to be able to accept this fact and not feel ashamed or be pitied. Nowadays, we have become too politically correct. At one time the word *cripple* was all we knew, but not now. Now we are handicapped or physically challenged or handicap–able or a person with a disability. I am glad society is aware of the great strength that people with disabilities have and has accepted what we have to offer, and I am not encouraging anyone to be so bold to refer to us as gimps. But in my world it's "hip to be *crip*" and I am proud to have been part of these games with all who participated. It was the day of the first time trials. I, along with my three teammates, waited and warmed up on the poolside. The joking had stopped. It was game time. All that we had worked for, all that I had trained for these last months was now soon to be challenged by others. We could feel the excitement building in the room. The scent of pool water and chlorine filled my nostrils. The smell of competition was in the air. As I entered the water, I thought of all the hours I had spent in the pool training for this moment. My first race was to be the backstroke, not my favorite, but we all had to swim at least three different strokes. My selections were backstroke, breaststroke and my preferred butterfly stroke.

My mind raced with memories of my arms stroking through the water. *Must keep your head straight, turn your body ever so slightly, long strokes, don't pull up too high or you suck water not air.* Holding on to the side of the pool, goggles in place, I looked down the colored bobbers edging my lane. Taking in deep breaths of air, I filled every bit of space in my lungs. I heard nothing but my breathing and the crack of the gun. *Here we go, man! No need to think any more just swim.*

Through the churning of the water I could hear the crowd roar. Looking up I counted each flag and breath that went by. *Don't stop until you hit the wall. Pull man! Pull!* As my forearm hit the top of the pool on the other side I knew I had made it. But was I fast enough? Finally, after what seemed likes hours, but in reality only a few minutes, I heard over the speaker: "Qualifying time for Richard Guerra, 44:3."

Hey, hey. That's me, I did it, I made the time under fifty seconds with a 44:3 time. Not bad for the first time out. But deep down I knew it was far from the time needed to win a medal in the nationals. No time to dwell on this though. I had to prepare for the next race, breaststroke. This race was the one that worried me, for I never really perfected this stroke, but I would give it my all.

At the crack of the gun, I set out in good form, my head bobbing up and down, taking good breaths, arms slicing forward and pulling hard sideways and back. It was all a matter of keeping a synchronized stroke, bobbing, and breathing. Too much of one or the other would cause you to stroke too hard, too fast. Then you would bob too high or low and instead of taking deep full breaths, you would take big gulps of water. I propelled myself through the water searching for the end.

This is not so bad; in fact I think I am winning. Go Rich go. Oh, the glory. I made it. I'm the champion of the breaststroke. How incredible! Oh, listen to the crowd. They are all standing and cheering: Rich! Rich! Rich! How sweet the sound, it's like I'm floating in the bliss. My name being called again: Richard! Richard! Can you hear me Richard?

As I opened my eyes to the sounds around me, I looked into the eyes of my coach as she held me on the side of the pool. Hey, what was she doing in the water? Wait I'm not in the water, I'm on the side of the pool cradled in her arms. And then I knew.

"Hey coach, bellied up didn't I?"

"Yes, but you sure were close. How, do you feel?"

"Not bad," I said, "had a little nap after drinking the pool."

Well, that was fun. What's next?

On to the third race, my baby, the butterfly. I put aside what had happened earlier. It happens to the best of us. And this must be true because my teammate, who qualified in backstroke, also bellied up during freestyle. It made one wonder what's up with this Manta Ray team? Were they really serious competitors or just a bunch of guys who frolic in the pool, the laughing stock of Marionjoy.

As my comrade and I prepared for the last race, we both knew we would have to prove ourselves and show our true colors. I looked down the eight lanes and then I glanced at my teammate three lanes over. With a nod and a look that said, *let's do it*. We both knew it was our time. At the end of the race the crowd stood and cheered and this time it was no dream. The swimmers who earlier bellied up not only placed first and second, but my teammate broke the state record. I was short by only a second–and–a–half. What a comeback and a true showing of will and desire. Will and desire, yes these are emotions that cannot be bought. They must be in you. And they are. Faith and hope are given to us all through the blood of Christ. One man I watched swam every race and even though he never won, he never stopped trying. In Seattle, a month later, I won a silver medal in the butterfly with a time of 31:03. I placed second in the country, beaten by the past champion of three years by only .23 of a second. I look back and put aside my feelings of how great I thought I was and remember the man who swam every race, never stopping, always pushing on; the man who had stubs for arms and stubs for legs, the quad amputee. I thank him and I praise God for the strength He gave him and me and all of us to continue on when we didn't think we could. To continue on with a never–ending faith, to continue on inch–by–inch, one foot at a time.

> And they were all amazed by the greatness of God.
>
> Luke 9:43 (KJV)

IT'S ONLY RIGHT

During the short time that I spent traveling to swim meets. Even as far as Hawaii where, I missed a bronze medal by one tenth of a second. I had the opportunity to meet other disabled athletes and share stories of living in an inaccessible world. These conversations led me to decide that it was time to end my career in the Wheelchair Games. There were two reasons for this.

First, at the age of twenty–six, I had spent two long years training, mostly alone, and I was getting a little tired of seeing nothing but bubbles and hearing nothing more than my breathing. The second and most important reason was that I now realized it was time to do more to bring awareness to the plight of people with disabilities in this country. There had been so many times during the past few years that the basic necessities, such as a wheelchair, as hard as it is to believe, were sometimes unobtainable. A good friend of mine became angry when he found out how hard it was to get a wheelchair. He was under the impression that the government provided this basic tool for mobility without any questions or hassles. How wrong he was.

There were many times when I found myself having to canvas local organizations such as the VFW or American Legions hoping to have a wheelchair donated no matter what condition or how old it may be. An old chair was better than no chair. And if it broke, well, no one paid for the costly repair. At one time I actually had a broken frame that was held together by piano wire. One time the frame on Pegasus broke and a Good Samaritan helped me out by welding the break. He welded the chair into a permanently open position I later discovered when I left his home and couldn't fold Pegasus in order to put him in the car.

It seemed that you had to be totally poverty stricken or extremely wealthy in order to have the equipment you needed. If your financial status were middle class, you fell through the cracks. The basic items cost more than a used car. The average cost of a basic wheelchair in those days, and there was only one major supplier and designer of this equipment, was between twelve hundred dollars and two thousand dollars for a manual and over sixteen thousand dollars for a powered chair. At the present well, you do the math. Just like anything else, the cost definitely hasn't gone down. And what's worse is the medical equipment suppliers always seem to base the price on supply and demand. Those disabled need the equipment and we have to pay whatever price they set. If you think about it, how can a brand new car cost less than a wheelchair? Makes one wonder.

After traveling to meet with many others with disabilities, I found many throughout this country shared these frustrations. This had to change. But how? One afternoon, I was pondering this problem that others and myself faced, and feeling disheartened, the Spirit of the Lord came to me. In those days, even though I did not always practice His Word, I believed in it. As you have read in previous chapters, God's love and saving grace was upon me many times, yet I still didn't always want to follow the right path.

Nevertheless, God was still doing His will. It used to amaze me how in a quiet moment or in the rush of the day you can hear His calling if you listen, believe, and have faith. I realized that I needed to work at making the public aware of the plight of the disabled in order to help those in need obtain the necessary equipment and even better to obtain it for free. Yes, that is what I would do. I would raise awareness and raise funds to achieve this end, and I would do this in the name of God. And knowing and believing at that time that it was God's will, I knew it was possible.

When I first spoke of this plan to others, many people told me that it was not possible.

"Why would anyone just give their hard–earned money to you to help people with disabilities even if they were in need?" they asked. Even my closest friend told me, "Rich, I know you really believe that this can be done and I'm not knocking your faith, but it won't happen. Why would anyone who isn't disabled and has no disabled family member care about you or anyone else? Only because I'm your friend do I care about you having a wheelchair, but that's about as far as it would go." For a moment there, he sounded convincing. I mean he was right. Why would anyone give me money just because I'm disabled? I thought that if I were a nonbeliever like him, and unfortunately many others, I would have agreed and dismissed the entire idea and chalked it up to just a dream of a desperate man who was in need.

But no, I was a believer, and I knew that God wanted this to happen. I knew then, as I know now, that He would give me the words I needed, and the words came. I will never doubt again. We will all become disabled either from age or accident, if we aren't disabled at birth. With these words, the premise of the American Handicapped Association (AHA) was founded and established. The goal was to aid, educate, and assist persons with disabilities. American people, in general, are a giving people and there are many that would like to assist those less fortunate, but they have to understand the problem. I started this journey by letting the public know why there was a need and how they could help me to help others. My first task was to write a letter to the public explaining how AHA was going help the disabled. I ended the message with, "God Bless you for caring."

There again my critics said, "You can't do that. You can't be signing things with God in them!" Well, you know what I think about *can't*, and I am so glad that with what little sense I had in those times I at least had enough not to listen to them. I continued to follow God's plan instead of my own, and I was not ashamed to praise His name to the masses, and I never will be. And you know what happened? It worked. In the first day of raising money, over six hundred dollars came in. Many of these donations were in the amount of five or ten dollars.

Never be ashamed to call out to God in a time of need or to give thanks openly. So many are. They are worried about what others will think or how people may stare, but if Jesus could do it, and imagine what he went through, then by his anointing we can. Look around the next time you have dinner in a restaurant. Look at all the families dining who say grace and give thanks for their meal at home (which we all should), but do not do it in public. Why?

Many years ago I met a big, powerful, bad man. He was one of those original biker men. He was so bad that bad men gave him gifts. He was a fierce fighter, a black belt in Karate, and feared by many on the streets. He cared about nothing and no one—surely not God. One evening in a drugged up, drunken stupor he crashed his big bad Harley and lay dying in the street, alone with no one to care about him. Why should they? He cared about no one. He was a bad man who lived a gangster life and trusted no one. As he lay there in a pool of his own blood, battered and broken, dying, he thought about how he had lived. When the ambulance arrived and the medics checked him for signs of life and found none, they prepared to slip his broken body into a bag and zip it up. But this man, who cared about nothing and no one. This man, who in a daily conversation, would never mention God. This man who lay dying enclosed in a plastic bag, at the last moment, when the last bit of light shone through the soon–to–be zippered bag. He believed that even as bad as he had been, and though he never praised God for his life, now at this moment in time, if he asked God to forgive him, He would. God will never forsake you if you believe in Him. At this time, he asked that God give these medics a sign to show them that he was still alive. He wanted to live and give praise and thanks for his life. He believed in God. The medics tagged and bagged his lifeless body and carried him to the ambulance. In the darkness of that plastic bag, his finger moved.

"Hey stop. This guy's alive!" he heard. As they unzipped the bag and the light shone through, he knew there was God. Now this big man, this man who cared about nothing and no one, this man who would never mention or give thanks to God in a normal day, this same man now preaches the Word of God every Sunday morning in his own church to the masses. He is not ashamed to let the world know that he believes. And just as God sent His only Son to us to share His word, we too have been appointed to spread His word throughout the land, throughout the nations, to share this great love with all we know and meet. To let the world know that in our darkest hour God is with us and will never forsake us and will forever light our way is our duty. Do not be ashamed to praise his name any time anywhere. I'm not. Are you? It's only right.

> Come and see the works of God, who is awesome
> in His deeds toward the sons of men.
>
> Psalm 66:5 (KJV)

THE TIME HAS COME

For a year I spent every waking moment thinking of how to raise money to fund the AHA. I tried many creative ideas and ventures all with the goal of creating awareness and assisting those in need of medical equipment. I started my own telemarketing firm, I had balloon launches, barbecues, I even had two college students trek across the United States on bicycles from Barrington, Illinois, to San Francisco, all to raise funds and create awareness.

It worked. Let me tell you about the first item AHA gave away, to illustrate how much need existed and how absurd the system was in the early Eighties.

An eighteen–year–old boy was sent to a nursing home for constant care. That is a horrific situation. Because his family lacked the means to make their home accessible, he was placed in a geriatric ward in a nursing facility. He received no rehabilitation services. If the situation were left unchallenged, he would grow old there. If that weren't bad enough, he was also in desperate need of an air cushion to sit upon to prevent the devastating breakdown of skin tissue on his bottom. Now at this time, an air cushion cost a mere one hundred dollars, but believe it or not, the insurance company denied him this item.

Can you believe that? An item that would prevent injury, an item that cost a stinking hundred dollars, was denied. When his skin did break down, which would definitely happen, they would with no problem pay for the cost of the extensive surgery that would follow, a surgery that could cost over ten thousand dollars. Now do you see why there was such a need for awareness and assistance? With nothing more than a few phone calls, AHA secured this cushion and presented it to this young man at no cost. How blessed we were to be able to do this and so much more.

As days became months and months turned into years, the needs increased and the battles grew bigger. The need to create awareness was never ending and this was the most important issue at hand. Until the American public saw the injustice that so many individuals with disabilities were facing, the likelihood of change was remote. At times it seemed that the battle would never end. How could one man hope to make a difference?

What I found, as time went on, was that many others were asking the same questions I was asking. So I began seeking out these individuals and agencies. I found many people who had a desire to raise awareness in these United States. Some groups I found were: Coalition of Citizens with Disabilities, Access Living, and, one of the most influential at that time, Americans Disabled Against Public Transit (ADAPT). The fun was about to start.

ADAPT was rallying all grassroots organizations throughout the country to fight against the America Public Transportation Authority (APTA), which at that time had not made buses or trains accessible for people with disabilities, even though the company made over seventy million dollars profit a year. They said that they could not afford to adapt buses and trains and claimed not enough people needed to use the service to justify the costs. Well, the disabled community didn't care whether one person used the service or a million. It was our right to have access to public transportation, and we aimed to fight for it.

Each year, even though the APTA stated they could not afford to spend money on making transportation accessible, they had enough money to wine and dine their employees for long weekends at beautiful resorts. ADAPT planned to disrupt these affairs and to demonstrate for the right to have accessible public transportation for all. One afternoon I received a phone call from a gentleman who was heading the local chapter in Chicago. He asked if I would participate in the upcoming rally in Phoenix, Arizona. Knowing that I needed to be involved, I said yes. For the next couple of months AHA and ADAPT raised the money to cover the cost of transportation for a hand-ful of members of the Chicago–land area to go to Phoenix. The flight to Arizona was without incident, except they wouldn't allow two passengers with electric wheelchairs to board because the airline was unable to accommodate them. Safety regulations prohibited their transporting the batteries for the wheelchairs. Imagine that! It is amazing how much we had to go through to ensure that the batteries would arrive with the wheelchairs. Then we had to put up with being hauled on the plane like baggage because aisles are too narrow. You would think that they could at least place us in the first rows. No, let's go all the way to the back of the plane, just to make it more exciting. Well I guess this was why we were going to attend this rally. After arriving at our destination and checking in the room, I had a chance to roam around and hear of past escapades of these demonstrators. *What am I in store for? Am I up to the fight?*

Seeing hundreds of people from across the country come together as one to fight for the same cause was amazing. We did not care what happened to us; we knew that we had to do something to change the attitude of this large agency. We had to fight for those who were unable to fight for themselves, no matter what the costs.

At the first meeting we talked about disrupting the events being held at the hotel, which housed people from the American Public Transportation Authority and blocking buses throughout the city. We thought disrupting transportation services for those who were able-bodied would open their eyes to the plight that those who were disabled were facing each and every day. This plan was intriguing, exciting, and somewhat frightening to say the least. More than likely we would be arrested for these actions. Now up to this point in my life, I had never put myself in the position to be arrested or spend a night in jail, and I really wasn't certain that I wanted to now. I shared my hesitations with the leader of our group, who in a short time became my dear friend. He was one of the strongest advocates I had ever met.

"Richard, there is nothing wrong in you feeling this way. It took me a time to be able to face this challenge and overcome any fear and I am sure, in time, the spirit will direct you. If you are uncomfortable when the time comes for the police to make arrests, just back away from the group." As he finished his last sentence on my palm, he squeezed my hand tightly. You see this man had to finger sign on my palm because he was blind, deaf, and in a wheelchair. With that squeeze, I felt a sense of strength and power surging through my being and I knew I could face this fear head on.

We had chosen to rally in Phoenix because the APTA was holding their convention there, but actually Phoenix was a leader in creating an accessible city. They even had some accessible public transportation. However, the APTA opposed allocating the funds necessary to equip all buses in the country with lifts, and they were doing all they could to make sure this wouldn't happen. Now at the time, I still hadn't grasped exactly what was going on. Why should I protest in a city that had accessible buses and risk the chance of being arrested and sent to jail? I would soon learn why, the hard way.

Every morning I looked forward to doing a workout in the gym to increase my strength and endurance, so I inquired as to the whereabouts of a local gym. Then I called the city bus to see if I could have transit to and from the downtown gym in a timely fashion the following morning. I wanted to work out and be back in time to attend the rally. I was told there would be no problem and the instructions would be carried out first thing in the morning.

The next morning I arrived at the bus stop near the hotel at half past six. Easy enough. At a quarter until seven, the first accessible bus was supposed to arrive. It was a beautiful warm morning, so I didn't mind the short wait. As the bus pulled up, I wondered how this lift would work. When the driver opened the door, I told him I was heading downtown and asked how I got on the bus.

"Sorry, this bus isn't equipped. An accessible one should arrive in another hour," he replied. He apologized for the bad information I had received, swung the door shut, and drove off.

An hour, huh, well that's not too long, I thought. Heck, someone just made a mistake. It's still a nice day. I'll just lift a little later and hurry back. No problem.

An hour and a half and two inaccessible buses later, the right one finally arrived. I sure was glad. It was getting a little warm outside.

"Hey, bus driver. I was told this bus will get me to the gym downtown. Correct?" I asked

"Well sir, it will get you downtown, but then you have to transfer to another bus to get to the gym. It will only be about a ten–minute or so wait, and then only about a fifteen–minute ride to the gym. Okay?"

"Okay," I replied. I mean what was another ten minutes, and the bus was air conditioned.

After getting off downtown, I asked a clerk at the terminal where I should wait for the next bus, the one that would be arriving in ten minutes.

"Ten minutes, who told you ten minutes? No sir. The next bus will be two hours from now. You see we only have one accessible bus on this line."

"Two hours. What do you mean two hours?" I exclaimed. "I was told I could get back and forth to the gym with no problem and now I have spent over three hours and traveled five miles and I am still not at the gym. And now I'm out of time."

Looking at me with a pitiless, condescending sort of gaze, he said, "Sir, I'm just so terribly sorry for the misunderstanding. Could I offer you a glass of cold water while you wait?" After explaining to him what he could do and where he should put the glass of water. I turned and started the five–mile roll back to the hotel. With each foot I rolled, I not only picked up steam, but also became more steamed. Upon entering the hotel, I looked around and no one was in sight except for two off–duty police officers that were assigned the task of making sure no gimps got out of line while in their fair city. As I looked around for someone I knew, I barked a question at them, while slamming the doors open.

"Where is everyone?"

I guess I must have looked a sight, because with a shocked look someone replied that they all went downtown.

Ah! Downtown? Downtown? I just came from downtown," I yelled as I turned and pushed through the doors to once again to head downtown.

As I rolled down the street, I realized how important it was to be part of the day's demonstration. I knew without a doubt what I was going to do once I arrived. On my way to the rendezvous point, I periodically asked people who passed by if they had seen any individuals in wheelchairs headed in the direction in which I was going. I wanted to be reassured that I was following the right path and soon would be amongst my comrades. As I turned the corner, I saw masses of people milling about. I approached the leader of my group.

"Colonel, what should I do," I asked.

"Block a bus," he replied, without a moment of hesitation.

With that, I headed toward the first bus I saw parked and rolled in front of it, much to the amazement and bewilderment of the bus driver, who looked down at me through the large windshield. There I locked my brakes and stood defiantly.

"Hey! You better move or I will run you over," the driver yelled, after a moment. Well, after what I had been through that day, I really did not care about his idle threats.

"Go for it," I yelled.

A large crowd was gathering and wondering what I would do next. I started explaining to the crowd why I had to be there and said I was not going to move, no matter what. After a few moments, a police officer arrived on the scene and told me that if I did not move, I would be arrested. This was the moment of truth. This was the time that I had thought about as I rolled those many miles back and forth. Now I had a choice to make. Would I go to jail or not? All I had to do was back away from the bus and go back on the sidewalk and I would be out of trouble. The look in the police officer's eye told me I was going to be arrested if I refused to follow his command. I looked back and forth from the crowd on the street to the disabled citizens. Then I knew what had to be done.

"Officer, I know you have a job to do. And so do I. So if you want to, arrest me. But, you're going to have to come and get me because I am not leaving. Got it?"

The crowd whooped and hollered, cheering me on. I experienced an incredible feeling even more exciting than when I won a race. It was more exciting than when I gave away a cushion. It was more exciting than anything I had ever experienced because I knew what I was doing and what I would go through were for a great cause. I could have never imagined that I would be a part of such an important event. And it felt great!

As a police officer and his partner approached me, I heard my comrades' yell out: "Don't worry, Richard. We'll be there with you and all will be well." I did not resist as the police escorted me from in front of the bus to a waiting van that was already occupied by a few others in wheelchairs. As I entered the van I heard someone in the back.

"Well I see you found a reason."

I had.

Now the interesting part began unfolding. None of the police stations were equipped to hold the number of disabled who were arrested, and none of us would agree to pay the small fine of fifty dollars to secure our freedom. Why should we? All of us were used to sitting around for hours on end in an uncomfortable situation.

The authorities came up with the bright idea to send us to the local state prison facility. Since we were charged with only a misdemeanor, they had to figure out how to keep us safe from the other inmates. This meant having to clear a cellblock just for us, then doubling up inmates in an already crowded prison. Let me tell you, this didn't sit well with the current tenants.

The more serious problem the warden and captains had to face were those with severe disabilities who would need more medical attention than the facility could provide. In addition, we were demanding additional mattresses for every bed so that we would not suffer any breakdown in our skin, not that this would happen to all of us, but they didn't know that. Combining all of the headaches we caused with constant chanting coming from the group and the local tenants, "Let our brothers go," weighed on the already frayed nerves of the staff. We held fast for seven days and nights. Finally, they could not take anymore and decided they really did not want to accommodate us any further. With a plea to the judge from the warden, we all found ourselves being released into the night.

We had stood up for the rights of the disabled across the country and even reaching out to our neighboring country Canada. We created a much needed awareness in the public, and continued to do so until the Americans with Disabilities Act was passed ensuring the right to accessible transportation and more. And now all the people knew the time has come.

> The Lord will not allow the righteous to hunger,
> but He will reject the craving of the wicked.
>
> Proverbs 10:3 (KJV)

ALIVE FOREVER MORE

Alive forever more. What a saying. What a beautiful thought to know that no matter what, we who are believers have the reassurance in knowing that God has granted us eternal life. As I approach the beginning of the end of this book, I ask myself if I have done what God has asked? Have I served Him as He requested of me from the onset of this book? As I thought of this, the Holy Spirit told me that I am not at the end, but at the beginning.

From the end of the last chapter to the beginning of this one, many years have passed. Many years I wasted walking in the desert alone, struggling and fighting for every inch of ground. Just as the Israelites walked for forty years to make a journey that should have taken only eleven days, I was searching for something that was always right in front of me if only I would have opened my heart and followed God's direction instead of my own. Now as I look back on the journey, I realize how often I suffered needlessly, and how lost I had become even when I thought I knew what I was doing. But there it is. There was the problem. *I thought* I knew where I was headed and had the plan down pat, only to realize and eventually accept that I knew nothing of the sort. Now I give God the glory and praise for protecting me and bringing me out of bondage. I walked aimlessly about never knowing what He had planned for me well before I was conceived. Once again, came the time when He was going to reveal His plan and make me listen.

June 22, 2003, was a warm summer morning. My bags were packed and stowed in the car as I prepared for the return trip home from a lovely visit to Chicago. We had celebrated the graduation of my dear niece, Tabitha, the day before with family and old friends. The smile on her face when she was recognized as a high honors student was a beautiful sight. She is one of my many nephews and nieces of whom I am proud. My love for them will never end and I thank God for the love they share with me. Prior to this trip I had taken an inventory of my life. My days consisted of going to work, entertaining friends, painting, playing music, and lifting weights, which made me look better, but not feel better in spirit. Even though I was without a mate at age forty–seven, I believed that someday this would change. I just had to be patient. I lived each day believing I would live the remainder of my life this way. In spite of how mundane my life had become, I accepted that I was better off than most and was glad of that.

I walked alone, not wanting to follow God's Word or direction, though I knew on many occasions that I would be better off if I did. But that was too hard. I would rather have the easy road, and more often than not, the wrong road.

There I had been at the party, looking good, all greased up with sun tan lotion, proud of my accomplishments. The many days of being in the gym made me feel good about myself or so I made myself believe. But as I prepared to leave that morning the heaviness in my heart was hard to ignore. This feeling was not a new one, but one that was played out every time I left the presence of my loved ones to make the long return trip home, alone. I was weary of being welcomed when I arrived home by the quiet *hello* of the walls. Donned with a smiling face, a mask that I wore quite well, I entered my sister's room to quietly say good–bye with a kiss and a hug. Stopping only for a brief moment to look into the room of my sleeping niece and thank God for her life as I watched her sleep.

"I love you and I'll see you around town like a dough-nut," I whispered. It was a phrase I only use with her. It was early morning, but the sun had already been up for a couple of hours. After a quick check of the gauges and locking of the seat belt, I headed home. The trip was usually long, boring, and uneventful most of the time, but this day was not the norm. In fact, it was going to be a day I would never forget, and another day I would survive only because of the Lord's blessings.

I drove about thirty miles and then decided, before settling in for the long haul, I would stop to use the handicapped facility at the last rest stop. I planned it to be a quick stop only using the restroom. Instead, in a few moments I would find myself fighting for my life.

Now take a breath. Think. What could possibly happen in a public washroom that could threaten my existence? Could it be an out–of–control car crashing into the building? Or a downed airplane, exploding into the building? A stray bullet from a gun battle between armed robbers and the police? Or could it be that the toilet upon which I was sitting in the handicapped stall broke off the wall throwing me violently upon razor–sharp shards of broken porcelain which severed a major artery leaving me to bleed to death on the cold tile floor? As absurd and preposterous as it sounds, the toilet in a public restroom nearly killed me.

Once again, in the blink of an eye, the course of my life changed forever. I lay on the floor in a puddle of water in a state of stunned disbelief. *What just happened? Where am I?* As I looked around, I realized that for some reason I was sitting in a pile of shattered porcelain locked in a handicapped stall. For one brief moment I was just mad that the toilet had broken free from the wall supports and I was drenched in water. The indignity of it all! Then I told myself not to make too big of a deal of the situation. I would get up, go to the car, get some clothes to change into and then tell the management what had happened. *Man! Wait till I get up.* Then, I looked down. The water in which I sat quickly turned crimson. I was bathed in a river of my own blood. *Okay, I know I have been cut. Now I need to get out of this stall so I can assess the damage.* This wasn't going to be easy for the door was closed with Pegasus blocking my escape. Meanwhile, my blood continued to flow, and the sight of this red pool induced panic.

I channeled my fear into a sense of urgency. In one quick motion I collapsed Pegasus and tossed him over and behind me enabling the door to swing inward. Now I had an escape route. I dragged myself out of the stall and into the open. A gruesome sight, I elicited gasps and screams from the other men in the restroom. I reached back and felt the stickiness of my life juices soaking my hands.

"Call 911!" I yelled. As I lay there, all I could see were the legs of men scurrying for the door. *They will get help. It will be okay.*

I lay waiting in the ever–increasing pool of my blood, gazing into the shiny whiteness of the cold tiled floor, expecting to hear the approaching footsteps of help. Instead I heard nothing. Time seemed to stop. Then everything stopped. Everything was gone, just gone, everything except the small spot before my eyes. Then I heard the hollow sound of my breathing and a thought came to me. *Well, you're bleeding a lot just like dying people in the movies. I wonder how long until I start getting cold, my lips go numb, and my vision blurs. Does that really happen before you die?* I gazed into the spot.

Hey! I feel cold, my lips are numb, and everything's getting fuzzy. I sure am tired. Then I knew—I'm dying. Is anybody here? Can anyone hear me? Maybe I'll go to sleep now. Sure is nice and quiet for a change. I need to sleep. My eyelids grew heavy and I waited to slip into a dream. Then, just like so many times before, I heard Him call.

"Hey, hey. Don't you go to sleep. Do you hear me? Wake up, wake up. You will not sleep. Not now, not yet, you have work to do. Listen to me. Fight. Do you hear me? I said, fight."

Suddenly my vision cleared. I heard the sounds of life around me, and I got mad—fighting mad! No, I will not die here. Not on this cold floor. Not alone. No, I will not let this be how my family will remember this day.

Then once again God sent one of His many angels of mercy to my side. She cradled my head in her arms and said help was on the way. Don't close your eyes, but stay awake. No problem, nothing I can't do. But they better hurry. Don't want to make me mad cause when I get mad I start to sweat and when I start to sweat I start to stink and then I get stinking mad. As I lay in this angel's arms, the identity of whom I never learned, I heard the sounds of the paramedics rushing to my side.

"Apply pressure, we have to stop the bleeding." "Let's get a pulse. What's your name?" "Richard." "Okay Richard, stay with us. Please we need to get some vitals. Can't get a pulse!" "Move! Do you hear me? Move. I'm dying." They understood. "Let's get him in the ambulance."

Ah yes, the ambulance, my first line of defense to beat death. As I lay on my stomach on the floor of the speeding vehicle, I could hear above the wailing of the siren, "Rich, stay with us. Can you hear me? Stay with us, only four more miles to go. Three, only three miles. Two. We're here, Rich, stay with me."

Okay, I'm here, but you got to hurry, man, cause I'm dying. Then I sensed those familiar fluorescent lights that lined the ceiling rushing past me. The sound of the cart crashing the door and the smell of bleach and antiseptics flooded my senses and I knew where I was.

"Help me," I said. "I don't feel very well. I'm dying." As the doctors and nurses worked at a feverous pitch, I lay hanging off the edge of the cot not wanting to move and interfere with their work, but I didn't know how long I could hold myself up. I was so tired you know. Then someone tucked a cushion below my head allowing me to relax.

Later I met the nurse whose lifted leg braced my head and provided a pillow. Soon I heard one of the most beautiful messages ever sent my way.

"Rich, we stopped the bleeding and we're pumping blood into you now." *Praise God I am going to live*! I could now let myself go to sleep, and I did. What felt like a moment later (that's what anesthesia will do), I awoke to the sight of my youngest and oldest sisters, Becky and

Sandra, standing over me. I reached for them both, held them tight and cried, because once again by the grace of God, in more ways than one, I was alive forever more.

> For thou hast delivered my soul from death, mine
> eyes from tears, and my feet from falling.
>
> Psalm 116:8 (KJV)

A NEW BEGINNING

I awoke in darkness. Only a quiet hum broke the silence in the room. My eyes fought to focus and I saw shadows through a thin curtain. "Hey, anybody here?" I croaked.

"Yes, Richard, we're right here. I'm coming," called a woman. She pulled the curtain back, and there she stood, Florence Nightingale, and I understood where I was. But I wanted to make certain.

"Where am I?" I asked.

"You're in a hospital and you're going to be fine now."

"Is there anybody here with me?"

"Yes, your sister. She will be right back." A moment later, I heard the voice of my youngest sister and then I felt her touching my arm. Her touch reassured me that all was well for the moment and I drifted back into a deep, deep sleep.

Many hours later I awoke to the sound of someone calling me.

"Rich, Rich, can you hear me? How do you feel?" I came to and saw one of the doctors who had helped save my life at the foot of my bed.

"Richard, you had a terribly serious injury. The glass that you fell on slashed you open and severed a vital artery. We weren't certain you were going to make it. You lost a lot of blood. We had given you over six pints, and then you lost some more during surgery when the artery tore open again. If you don't have faith in God, well you ought to now because it is really a miracle that you survived." I lay there with my eyes closed, trying to shut out the pain.

Doc, you don't know how right you are, I thought.

"We have you on a life–monitoring system, Rich, and we'll be checking your blood pressure every fifteen minutes for awhile. We have you sedated with morphine because I'm certain you must be in a lot of pain even though you aren't screaming, and by all rights you should be. You aren't showing signs of pain. On a scale of one to ten can you tell me how much you hurt?"

"One to ten, huh? Well Doc, I would have to say twelve. Yeah, twelve."

"How is that, Rich? How could I tell you hurt so much?"

"Well Doc, look at me. As I talk to you, my eyes are closed tight. Now, I would like to open them, but I can't bear to do that. Also I feel like my teeth are being pulled out of my gums slowly, roots and all. And on top of that, my head feels as if it is going to explode any minute. So Doc, don't think that just because I have paralysis, I don't hurt. It just means I feel pain in a different way." And my dear readers, I think you would agree pain is pain no matter how or where you feel it. Right? "All right Rich, can I get you anything?" "No thanks, Doc. Hey, Doc?" "Yes?" "Thanks." He smiled humbly. "You get some rest now."

Day and night I was under the ever–watchful eyes of many nurses who held a never–ending vigil to assure that my blood pressure did not drop, for that would mean that my artery had reopened. Thank God, this never happened. As I lay in the hospital bed, many thoughts came to me. The most frightening was how close I had come to dying. This fact became even clearer to me when doctors and nurses who weren't even caring for me popped in to see me. Hearing of the tragedy that had befallen me, they came to express their best wishes and to tell me I was a miracle. One evening, a nurse sat with me for a moment and asked about the accident. As I was reliving the horrible accident, I experienced yet another miracle. All the fear and pain and horror that I had experienced was flowing out of me. The nurse hugged me and with tears in her eyes.

"God has blessed you with another chance at life, Richard, and has a reason for you to be here." I knew what she said was true and the two of us cried together. All the fright was gone and my life was more precious to me than it had ever been before. I didn't know what was in store for me, but I knew that my life was forever changed.

The injuries I had sustained were horrific. The broken porcelain had cut a huge peace symbol less the circle into my left buttocks. It had torn close to my rectum. Tissue the width of a scalpel was the difference between independence and being dependent on a medical device to empty my bowels for the rest of my life.

The first time after the accident that I faced sitting on the toilet, I was gripped with fear. What would happen? Would this simple natural act become my downfall and eliminate my independence forever? I tried so hard to suppress the need to relieve myself, but eventually nature took over. To my tremendous relief I suffered no further damage. The fear of further damage occurring has only recently been put to rest, several years after the accident. The fear of sitting on a suspended toilet however remains. I don't think it will ever completely leave me. I was finally released from the hospital when I no longer needed intensive care, but I was far from being well. One of my sisters, Margo, came to pick me up and take me to her home. I would stay with her until I could return to my own home. The sliding glass doors of the hospital opened and I was wheeled to the waiting car. A warm summer breeze tickled my skin. I looked up at the heavenly blue sky and a more peaceful blue I couldn't recall. I looked around and seeing the world as if for the first time was overwhelmed with an inexplicable joy.

"Bro you know this was almost three strikes and you were out," my sister said, as we began our drive home.

"No Sis, I think what I did have was four balls and a walk," I replied without a moments hesitation.

"What do you mean?"

"Well, when I broke my neck that was the first time I could have died. Then remember when I went Code Blue? That was the second time and then when my appendix ruptured that was the third time. Now this time. So I would have to say I had four balls and I walked, right?"

She agreed, and we continued on with smiles on our faces and gratitude in our hearts.

The next several weeks my dear sisters and family comforted and cared for me. It was trying for all of us, but they never once wavered from the task at hand and cared for me until I was once again able to care for myself. The majority of the days were spent in a prescribed, drug–induced state in order to keep pain free and rested. More than a month later I thought I was ready to return to my own home and live alone once again.

I drove home in a trance. My mind seemed to become a movie of sorts as all the events of the past weeks filtered through me. When I passed the site of the accident, I began to cry and had to pull over to regain my composure. Though I still dislike passing this site, it is easier than it used to be. Time and faith will do that and I am grateful for this. Though the ordeal that I had to overcome was horrific, the whole experience was not without its rewards. God never gives us more than we can handle and He is always with us as we fulfill the life He has planned for us since the beginning of time.

Now you may ask yourself what rewards could come of such a horrible experience? Let me tell you, I asked myself this question numerous times throughout the months that followed. As time went by, I slowly regained my strength. In fact, it took almost a year for me to really feel strong again. Losing as much blood as I lost takes a big toll on a body, and even though I was given blood, I found that it takes the body a long time to replenish the power of its own blood cells. I spent many days sitting on my deck looking forward to the time when I would be able to move from one end of the deck to the other without being winded and totally exhausted, let alone lift weights again. However, through this period I was made to be still, reflect, listen, and be thankful.

As I sat staring at the flowered bushes and watching the bees and the butterfly's going about their daily God–given tasks with ease and peace, I realized how stressful and cluttered with unnecessary fears and problems my life had been. I believe my life felt this way because I was not seeking to follow God's direction, but my own. Even after everything I had been through, I still hadn't sought to understand what God wanted of me. No, instead I just selfishly lived each new day as my own. Soon though, God would put an end to my thinking this way. I had to spend a great deal of time lying on my side so as not to aggravate the wound as it healed. Avoiding one physical problem just created another though as bad if not worse. The constant pressure wore on my skin and I developed a decubitus ulcer, in lay terms, a breakdown in the skin.

This situation is dangerous for people who suffer paralysis. This type of wound becomes an open sore because the skin tissue dies from the inside out. Since the tissue has died, new tissue does not regenerate as rapidly as that of a normal wound making it more susceptible to infection and all the illness this brings. So now, on top of everything else, I had to contend with this pain and by no means was this fun.

Day after day, month after month I continued to fight to heal these wounds. At one point I thought the best approach would be to stay off Pegasus and lie in bed on my stomach to give the wounds total relief from pressure for however long it may take. It had to be done. This task was not easy living alone and fending for myself. I still had to feed myself, bathe myself, and keep the house at least somewhat clean. So even though I spent many hours in bed, I still had to endure the pain of sitting on an open wound a few hours a day. These hours were short, but all I would allow myself to have. In an entire twenty–four hour period, I would be up for no more than four hours.

Just as surely as anyone in solitary confinement, this routine took its toll on me physically, and even more, mentally. As I lay in bed hurting and alone hour after hour, day after day, week after week, the anger grew. Yes, I was angry; angry that I had to endure all of this pain and suffering because of the lack of care and maintenance of a public facility that was supposed to be a safe haven for a weary traveler. Instead it was the site of my worst nightmare. I was also angry because those who were at fault tried to dismiss it as an accident to dodge their responsibility. I knew in time they would be brought to justice and made to pay for their error, but this future scenario did nothing to make the present any easier to endure. In fact, it made it worse. Unable to do anything immediately to those who allowed this to happen, I slowly turned my anger upon the one who loved me the most, God.

How could He do this to me? Why? Why would He make me go through all this again? Haven't I had enough? What does He want from me? What? And then I knew something that I have always known, something that I should have always been doing, something that I did not want to do, and that was to serve Him! This realization came to me only after He had made me to bow down before Him, to cry out for His grace, to believe with all my heart and soul that He loves me and will heal me and guide me if I will just listen and obey. To serve Him with an open heart was all He asked. In return, I would be rewarded with all the blessings He has to give. And by the grace and will of God, this day came.

For many weeks I struggled to believe and to find some answer to why this was happening and to understand what I had to do, but no answers came. I found only frustration, sadness, and anger. I realized I could not go on this way and if I didn't seek help, I would surely lose my mind.

In the quiet of the night, in the darkness of loneliness, I called out to God.

"Please Lord, if you want me to stay in this bed I will. If it is for twenty–four hours straight I will endure. But I don't believe that this is want you want of me. Yet, I don't know what I should do. Please save me, Lord. My need for you is great. I know I am lost without you."

He heard and He listened and then through His love He made me to hear.

The countless hours of lying in bed with nothing to do but stare into the bleakness of a television screen numbed my senses. Night became day and day became night. One night I awakened in the wee hours of the morning from a restless sleep. I sat and stared into the darkness. No, there is no way that I am going to start the day this early looking at the TV. I tried to convince myself to go back to sleep even though I knew sleep was hopeless. Then with a sigh of despair the inevitable happened. I pressed the power button on the television remote.

With a sense of dread, I watched as the screen became light. I focused on the show that appeared. The program playing was a female minister speaking of God's Word. For a moment I considered changing the channel, but instead I continued to watch and actually listened to the entire show. At the end of the program I felt a sense of peace and with no other thought went back to sleep for a minute.

The next day was a repeat of the previous day. It passed by slowly, minute after long minute and hour after long hour, until once again night fell. I went to sleep, but woke to find myself in the same predicament I had been in twenty fours hours earlier.

Frustrated, I sat once again in the darkness. Oh no. Is this what it has come to? Is God not hearing my pleas? Does he not care? With that, the light of the screen appeared and what came into view was somewhat shocking to me. There, once again, was this woman talking about God, about all the love and grace He has for me. Me! Can you believe it? She was talking about God's love for me. I listened and I heard.

This is really incredible. How can this be? This woman is talking what I am going through. When the program ended, I marked the time, and as I drifted back to sleep, I felt different. Calmer and empowered, yet I also experienced a feeling of need and want.

The next day, I looked forward to the end of the twenty-four hours so I could arrive once again at this peaceful place. I did. Every morning for the next week I looked forward to the wee hours when the TV would wake me to hear God's Word ministered to me by Joyce Meyer. My mornings were transformed. Each day started with hope, not despair. Each day I wanted to hear more and as crazy as it may sound, I longed for the day to end so it could start anew with another teaching.

October 1, 2004, was a Friday I will never forget. I had just drifted back to sleep when my phone rang. Since it was still quite early in the morning, I thought this could not be good news. On the other end of the line was my dear niece, Denise, calling from afar. This right away brought me to attention because a call from her was not an everyday occurrence, especially this time of morning.

"Uncs," she said. She never called me uncle. "I'm sorry to wake you so early, but it was most important that I called."

Oh no. Here it comes, bad news, I thought.

"Is everything okay?" I asked.

"Yes Uncs, nothing's wrong, but I need to tell you something and please you have to listen. I have been up for many hours already and while on break at work the Holy Spirit came to me and told me I must call you."

Knowing my niece and her devout faith in God I said, "Okay. Honey I'm here I'm listening. Go ahead."

"Uncs, you have to write a book and you have to start today. And don't worry, God is going to be with you because He wants you to write this book."

I'm glad to hear that because I surely have never written a book, I thought.

"He wants you to write about your experiences being disabled and what you have gone through, because people with disabilities that read this book will come to know

His Word. And those people that are not disabled that read it will come to know His Word." Let me tell you, by this time I was definitely awake and taking notice. "The Holy Spirit also told me to tell you that He wants you to keep a Bible close by, because as you type, He will want you to share a message and will guide you when that time comes. And Uncs, this is most important. You must go back to church and you must do these things now." And like any good salesman she continued to share more good reasons why this was so important. As much to my amazement as hers, I interrupted her.

"Okay. Yes, I will write this book and I will start today." There was a moment of silence on the line.

"Really Uncs?"

"Yes, I will," I said. "And I have just the title for the book. It will be called *Four Balls and Walking*."

With a squeal of delight she said, "Uncs, you don't know what blessings are in store for you because of you wanting to be obedient to God's request. Thank you for listening."

After saying our goodbyes, I sat for a moment soaking in what had just happened, not understanding but knowing that I must do this task. Thinking back I had no doubt that this book was going to be a reality. So I began not only writing a book, but also transforming my life, learning about and understanding the grace of God and how quickly He can change your life.

My thoughts were full of ideas of how I would perform this task. I felt like Ebenezer Scrooge waking on Christmas morning realizing he hadn't missed it.

I felt just as giddy as he felt. Type, type, this is what I must do. How? It's most important that I stay in bed, but how will I type if the computer is in the other room? Move it!

I stared at the small space at the foot of my bed. Yeah, I bet the desk will fit in here. I'll just need some help getting it moved. Even though I knew it was early and most of my friends would be heading for work or just starting their day, it did not matter. I had to have their help and I knew they would help even if the request was strange. I decided not to tell them why it was so urgent that this be accomplished this evening, but rely on their friendship knowing they would help without question. At that time I still was not a true believer in God's works, because if I had been I would have proclaimed God's glory and His request. Instead I worried that my friends would think I was losing my mind because I had been bed–ridden for too long. Nevertheless I called and made the request.

God started to work through me immediately. My friends didn't need an explanation for the urgency of having this done in one evening. They not only came and moved the computer, but also they rewired the bedroom to adapt to the computer lines. If you can believe this, the entire desk fit with only inches to spare at the foot of my bed. Having the computer there would enable me to type and yet still heal in the bed. Praise God, for He had already started to answer my prayers.

Remember how I had asked for Him to give me something more to do than just lie in the bed? In the year and a half after starting this book and devoting my life to following His Word and direction, more blessings arrived, some greater than I could have imagined. Every day I still stand in wonder and awe of His love and grace that He gives us each and every day if we choose to believe and be obedient to His direction. I had never lived His way before, but I will from now on because I have learned that being obedient to God does not make one weak, but to the contrary, it makes one strong. I also learned that the more you wish to be close to God and the more you follow Him, the more the enemy will try to stop you.

The next morning when I awoke the only thought on my mind was starting God's book. Everything was set. The computer was right in front of me and I could type while in bed. What a great Saturday this was going to be, or was it? Before starting I wanted to freshen up and have breakfast. As I transferred on to Pegasus from the bed, I couldn't believe what had happened. I had two flat tires. Well, let me tell you, wheelchair tires are just like bike tires. After much use the tread will wear away leaving the tire susceptible to punctures and slow leaks, but these tires were new and I had been up in Pegasus the night before and had not traveled outside the house since. While occasionally one tire went flat, never in all the years that I have used a wheelchair had I experienced two flats at the same time.

What am I going to do? In the past, I probably would have cursed the day, but this time I was calm. I experienced no panic or anxiety, but intuitively knew what to do. The man who often repaired Pegasus at the shop was also a good friend and I knew in an emergency he would come to my aid. I reached him at home and explained my predicament. He asked if I would be able to get to my car. I assured him that even though I was rolling on rims, I could make it the short distance to my car. With that he told me to meet him at the shop and he would fix the flats while I waited. So off I went.

Upon examination of the tires, he was just as perplexed as I was. He had put on the new tires.

"Rich, I checked the rims and tubes to see if there were any leaks and filled the tires with air and they're just fine," he said. We both sat there scratching our heads trying to figure out why the tires went flat. He asked if anything out of the ordinary had happened the previous night. I shared with him what had transpired since Friday morning and he looked at me and made a shocking remark.

"Rich, maybe the devil was trying to stop you from writing and he figured if he ruined your day you wouldn't type." Ah yes, I had forgotten about him. But could this be true? My dear readers, you must decide just as I have to decide, is the enemy trying to destroy us as much as God is willing to save us? I believe he is, but even more, I believe that he will never succeed as long as we believe in God's power and grace. How about you?

As I drove back home, I pondered what had happened. Since I really had no explanation, I decided that I would not concern myself with it but continue on with my day. As I have grown in faith and learned more about the wonders of God and the Holy Spirit, I see now that the Holy Spirit had already been working within me and preparing me for this task many months before. All I could think of was doing God's bidding no matter what, and yet up to this point, I had really never been true to God's ways. You know I talked the talk, but never truly walked the walk in faith. Now everything seemed so clear to me. When I arrived home, I knew what had to be done and I started preparing to type the first chapter.

As I said a moment ago, the Holy Spirit had already started me on this task way before this day. During the spring of the year, after having been given the chance to live again, I had spent many hours sitting in the warmth of the sun trying to figure out what had happened. I had thought about all the trials I had gone through up to this time, and I remembered that years ago I had written about the first days when I suffered the spinal cord injury. A young man who had faced a devastating injury, I thought I should record the experience, why I don't know. It must have been that I had a lot of time on my hands and many lonely hours counting the spots on the ceiling tiles. Who knows? But this handwritten chapter of no more than a few pages, now discolored by time, had stayed with me through all the years and travels and moves of the last thirty years. It was still safely tucked away in a tattered box that once housed a Bible given to me by my sister.

Deep in the far reaches of my mind, I knew it was always with me even though I had not seen or read it in many years. I really never cared to, because I knew what was in store. I had a compelling need to read these words again, yet something kept stopping me from opening up the plastic bag in which the sheets were stored. They lay on my nightstand for many weeks. I somehow knew that it was most important that I read them, but I didn't want to relive the past.

I fought to ignore them as long as I could. Then the time came when, reluctantly, I grabbed the bag and prepared to open it. I felt as if there was some sort of monster inside. As I stared at the bag, I noticed that all the pages had been folded in half, so not to expose the words. To my amazement when I turned the bag over, of all the pages, one of them had been folded in the opposite direction exposing the letters of a sentence. It read: "The cords of the grave coiled around me; the snares of death comforted me. In my distress I called to the Lord; I called out to my God. From His temple He heard my voice; my cry came to His ears" (II Samuel 22:6). At that moment I sat in awe. I was overwhelmed with a renewed sense of the Holy Spirit.

Of all the things that could have possibly material-ized at that moment in time, of all the things that were needed to comfort me, of all the things that I could have ever imagined taking place, never could I have imagined this to be taking place in my life now. These words. God's words were revealed to me. God's words that I had hid-den away for so many years in the dark now came into the light. Lighting my way. Strengthening me. Preparing me for a new way of thinking. It was a new way of living and a new life. And with that, I now had the strength to continue on, to read what had been written so many years before.

As I read, I felt like I was reading of someone else, not myself. How could a young man who was enduring such pain and sorrow ever write these feeling and thoughts? Who was this person? Then I remembered who he was. He was a young man who had heard the word of God and believed. He was a young man who trusted without ques-tion in these words unlike the man that I had become. I was a man who had fallen away from God's direction, a man who cared only of fleshly desires that the world had to offer, a man who was lost and did not even know it. By the power of God, this man has been given a renewed life. He has been given the opportunity to serve God by sharing his pain and sorrow, joy, and happiness. He is a man who has been made aware that he can, and will, write a story of God's glory. And those words written by a young man so many years ago are now the beginning of this book.

Now you may think this is the end of the story, but it really has only started. That same afternoon, as if what had transpired in the past forty–eight hours wasn't enough, I received a call from some dear friends asking if I would like to attend church with them the following morning. Much to their amazement, without a moment of hesita tion, I blurted out, "Yes! Yes I would love to go to church with you. What time? When? I'll be there." It would not have mattered where, when, or how far, because I knew I was going to go to church. And I did.

My dear readers, since that day I have believed, learned, listened, followed, and served my God willingly. By doing this I have been blessed so that I may be a bless-ing to others in many ways, more than I could have ever imagined possible. My days are now filled with peace and joy. A life filled with a new beginning.

> Then the Lord stretched out His hand and touched my mouth, and the Lord said to me, "Behold I have put my words in your mouth."
> Jeremiah 1:9 (KJV)

A special note from my dear mother–in–law Mama Ruth

My Special Friend
I have a friend I go no place without him. He's my companion from morning to night. You might say he and I are tight. He's really not heavy nor is he light, but without him I would be a fright. Now there are some places we cannot go and this makes me mad, you know.

My body sometimes says I can't you see, but my pride says just watch me. He has a name, but he can't talk. Yet we still can go for a walk.

My friend has two wheels as down the road we go. Pegasus is the name I gave him, you know. For when I was a lad just nineteen years of age I jumped in shallow water, forever to change. But I still tell myself there is no reason to be living in gloom. Put a smile on your face and let your spirit zoom.

Because Jesus lives in my heart and I know him as my friend, that's Christ the Son. Now all I ask is for Jesus to let me live long enough to not die young.

—Ruth Thunhorst